Humor
That
Works

D1280004

Humor That Works—Advance Praise

"Funnily enough, this book is hilariously useful. Think of it as a practical playbook that helps you reconsider the way you do things and results in heightened levels of happiness. Every leader should read this book, work with the tools provided, and get serious about making people smile."

PHIL M. JONES

Sales Coach and best-selling author, *Exactly What to Say*

"If Brian Regan and Warren Buffett had a baby... and that baby could write a book... it would be this book! Drew's *Humor That Works* gives real-world examples of how humor increases effectiveness and job satisfaction and sets the stage for more meaningful human interactions that will bring benefits to the workplace and beyond. As Drew writes, 'To be more human at work, use more humor at work.'"

TIM MCGILLOWAY

Global Solution Manager, Procter & Gamble

"Pay attention to the strategies Drew shares in this fantastic book—filled with ideas on how to help you incorporate humor as a daily habit in your personal and professional life. His ideas will drive productivity, credibility, and connectivity. A must-read for every leader and a great gift for every team member!"

NEEN JAMES

Attention Expert and author, *Attention Pays*

"In today's world we are constantly bombarded by noise, a noise that manifests itself as pressure, process, and back-to-back meetings. Too easily noise prevails. Drew, with *Humor That Works*, shows us we can take control. Even better, we can have a good time doing so. Reading this book is eye-opening, not just for what it reveals about the power of humor, but also because it shows how we can master it."

MARY TAFURI
Chief Sales Enablement Officer, IBM Cloud

"Drew Tarvin's expertise as the world's first humor engineer shows in *Humor That Works*. Taking you through the what, why, and how of humor, Tarvin will make a believer out of anyone skeptical that humor is a must-have skill in the workplace. This book will level up your efficiency and effectiveness with unique strategies you don't find in your average business book."

DORIE CLARK
Adjunct Professor, Duke University Fuqua School of Business, and author, *Entrepreneurial You* and *Stand Out*

"The evidence is irrefutable: humor has improved my humanitarian work. Thanks to Drew Tarvin's seriously fun approach, I can bring science and innovation to overburdened disaster managers and the vulnerable communities they serve, in memorable and surprisingly effective ways. *Humor That Works* is about designing and deploying smart communication—effective and evidence-based, well beyond mere entertainment. Drew helps us understand that there is a process to harnessing humor in your workplace."

PABLO SUAREZ, PH.D.
Associate Director for Research and Innovation, Red Cross Red Crescent Climate Centre

(AN)DREW TARVIN

Humor That Works

The Missing Skill for Success and Happiness at Work

PAGE TWO
BOOKS

ISBN 978-1-989025-83-3 (paperback)
ISBN 978-1-989025-84-0 (ebook)

Page Two
www.pagetwo.com

Cover photo by Rachael Lee Photo
Illustrations and exquisite hand modeling by Andrew Tarvin

Web: drewtarvin.com
Email: drew@drewtarvin.com
Social: @drewtarvin

Agenda

* * *

0 Introduction 1

I **The What and Why of Humor**

1 Humanity's Desperate Need for Humor 15

2 Why Choose Humor 29

3 Defining Humor That Works 45

4 The Skill of Humor 63

II **The How of Humor**

5 Humor and Execution 83

6 Humor and Thinking 103

7 Humor and Communication 119

8 Humor and Connection 137

9 Humor and Leadership 155

10 Success and Happiness at Work 173

III **Debrief**

Acknowledgments 195

No Excuses Resources 199

Sources 203

0
Introduction

• • •

I AM A NERD. If you're wondering what type of nerd, the answer is "Yes." Computer, math, sci-fi, video game, Star Wars, Star Trek, Star Bucks... All of the above. Specifically, I'm an engineer. Like most engineers, I am allergic to the sun (I use SPF building), and I'm obsessed with efficiency; I believe the word efficient should be one syllable.

Ever since I can remember, I've tried to do things as efficiently as possible. Or even since before I can remember, because I was born three weeks early. Even in the womb, I was thinking, *I've got things to do. Let's go, Mom!* In kindergarten, my mom told me I had to choose what I wanted people to call me. Did I want to go by Andrew, Andy, or Drew? Five-year-old me chose Drew, and I'd like to think it was because it's the most efficient form of my name.

In high school, I decided that smart for me was getting a 93 percent in all of my classes, because 93 percent was the lowest grade you could get and still get an A. If I got a 94, a 95, or—worst case—a 100 percent, I was upset, because it meant I did more work than I had to do.

For college, I went to the Ohio State University, where I received three educations. Not three degrees—I'm no doctor even if the first two letters of my name are Dr—but three educations.

The first education was my actual degree: computer science and engineering, where I learned how to think, how to develop processes for efficiency, and how to program a robot we named Mordecai and the Dancing Yiddish Clowns. I learned the wonders of project plans, critical path schedules, and that "scope" isn't just a mouthwash. And I learned the technical skills I needed to complete tasks.

The second education was in becoming a resident advisor, where I learned how to better interact with fellow human beings, how to engage with people on multiple levels, and how to use 47 meal swipes in the last three days of the semester. I learned the importance of emotional intelligence, empathy, and empanadas (there was a good Mexican place near campus). And I learned the relationship skills I needed to manage a job.

The third education was in starting an improv comedy group, where I learned how to make people laugh, how to listen more intently, and how to turn any suggestion into a pun. I learned the power of *yes and*, comedic structure, and confident delivery. And I learned the humor skills I needed to enjoy a lifetime.

After graduating from Ohio State, I started working at Procter & Gamble as an IT project manager, where I managed the portal (a fancy word for website) for modeling and simulation in upstream research and development, led multi-million-dollar projects for a $350-million brand, and became a trusted advisor for the Prestige sales team because of my analytics skills and boyish charm (but mostly my analytics skills). I realized along the way that the success I was having at P&G—the awards, promotion, opportunity, and thorough enjoyment of what I was doing—was a result of my three educations at Ohio State.

Computer science taught me to find the best way to do things. I read top-rated business books and learned how to get things done, how to win friends and influence people, and how to habitually be highly effective seven ways. I consistently sought feedback from my managers so I could iterate improvement, and I deconstructed my work into its most basic components so I could do it as efficiently as possible.

My experience as a resident advisor taught me to manage people up, down, and across the organization. I recognized that my success was not going to be solely from my technical skills; I had to manage the human component of work. I started playing the politics of the corporate world, taking on certain projects for visibility, and saying, "Let's circle back on this" when I never wanted to talk about a subject ever again.

And improv taught me to use humor. I realized people were far more likely to do something if it was fun, myself included. I found ways to insert funny and/or embarrassing pictures of myself in my presentations, added jokes at the ends of emails (which I aptly named PS for the Pun Script), and started an internal blog that revolved around these three things—engineering, emotional intelligence, and humor.

After two years of exploring these concepts internally at P&G, I started sharing them with non-Proctoids (a.k.a. the general public) through a blog called *Humor That Works* in 2009. And just like at P&G, the ideas hit home with people as a way to be more productive, less stressed, and happier. Three years later, I left P&G to become the world's first humor engineer, combining my three educations with my experience at one of the world's top companies to solve corporate problems using humor.

Since then, with my team at Humor That Works, we've helped more than 25,000 people from more than 250 different organizations from all around the world use humor to achieve success and happiness in the workplace. We've deconstructed both work and humor and put them back together in a way that is more engaging, entertaining, and effective. We've built a series of resources to allow individuals to take back their work, to find ways to love what they do—and to actually do it better.

And now we have this thing you're holding in your hands, reading on your screen, or listening to me read like a bedtime story where everyone worked happily ever after. This book is for anyone who wants to join the humor-engineering revolution to get better results and have more fun.

I'm glad you've joined us.

About the Book

One of the things we've learned from the 500-plus events we've done around the world is that humor is not a one-time thing. It's not something you learn from a single talk and not something you benefit from by doing a single time.

The real benefits come when humor becomes a habit, when it becomes part of *how* you get things done, win friends and influence people, and habitually be highly effective seven ways. (Yes, I'm sticking with this joke.)

To learn about humor, you could focus on the theories of what makes us laugh, which Peter McGraw does brilliantly in *The Humor Code*. You could explore the reasons humans started using humor, like Dennett, Hurley, and Adams cover in *Inside Jokes*. You could even read a guide on how to become a stand-up comedian, like Judy Carter's *The Comedy Bible*. This book doesn't do any of that.

The purpose of *this* book is to provide you with a compact, cohesive resource for understanding the what, why, and how of using humor at work. The goal is to make you a better business-person, not a humor academic, anthropologist, or stand-up comedian. It builds on some of the most important business skills relevant in today's work environment (e.g., growth mindset, psychological safety, verbal fluency), teaches techniques for leveraging humor, and is centered on helping you take action to improve your work immediately.

While you will learn ways to improve your humor skill, the book is not specifically about how to be funnier. It's about how to be effective-er. At the end of the page, this is a business book, not a humor book.

That being said... it is a business book about humor, so humor will be had. If you're familiar with what we do at Humor That Works, or if you've seen me speak, you know what I mean. In fact, you may even notice a few of the same examples from my talks shared here. You're not experiencing déjà vu: it's because they work (case in point: I will talk about my grandmother). There will also be plenty of new examples and concepts to further exemplify effective humor (case in point: I will talk about a space knight).

There are stories, anecdotes, charts, graphs, at least one reference to *Doctor Who*, and definitely more than a few puns. There is also a smattering of footnotes that you should definitely read.[1] Everything in this book is here to make a point, demonstrate a technique, or make you smile.

For example, the introduction to this book is very intentional. You might think it's narcissistic to start a business book all about yourself. And it is. But the story of how I got to where Humor That Works is today is important, because it's a preview of what you are about to experience.

---

1 Why? Because my footnotes are mostly additional resources that can help you even more. You can also find all the suggested resources in one spot: gethumor.org/resources. If you're looking for the sources to various studies or claims, those are all in the back of the book under Sources.

We're going to take work apart and then build it back up again, choosing humor as the key *how*. We're going to focus on the mindset required to understand and manage the hardest component of any workplace: humans. And we're going to cover actionable strategies to achieve specific workplace goals by using humor.

And we're going to have fun doing it. One thing I've learned in my 10-plus years doing this is that success at work and in life requires more than just having the technical skills to do your job. Yes, you have to be good at what you do. But you also have to be good at how you do it.

In the mortal words of Leeroy Jenkins, let's do this.

Disclaimer

. . .

NOTE, SINCE THIS is a business book about humor, our lawyers ask that you please read the following disclaimer and hit "Agree."

Information contained in this book (hereinafter referred to as the "book") is presented "as is," without warranty of any kind. In particular, Humor That Works, its employees, officers, members, fans, friends, acquaintances, and people who have ever used the phrase "humor that works" make no warranties, representations, expressed or implied, as to the fitness for a particular purpose or merchantability of any product, apparatus, service, image, idea, font, joke, pun, or story, or the completeness or accuracy of any processes, methods, memorized text, or other information contained, described, disclosed, implied, not implied, inferred, referred, or thought about herein for every job ever.

Additionally, the following disclaimers hold true for the aforementioned book that follows:

1. Humor That Works makes no claims that it has solved every problem or has the perfect, one-stop-shop, one-size-fits-all, no-holds-barred, guaranteed-to-work-all-the-time solution but rather is presenting information to help push forward the ideas and theories presen-ted here.

2. This book is not your standard fare, taxi fare, or laissez-faire when it comes to business books. This book will be fun. This fun will not hinder the reader's ability to comprehend, understand, retain, or otherwise use the valuable content that follows. In fact, it is likely said fun will enhance the reader's ability to comprehend, understand, retain, or otherwise use the valuable content that follows.

3. While Humor That Works employs smart, talented, educated, charming, and sexy people, Humor That Works also understands that the reader is smart. Humor That Works does not pretend to be an expert in the field(s) in which the reader is working. In fact, Humor That Works can almost guarantee that Humor That Works does not know nearly as much as the reader about the company, industry, region, building, customers, clients, users, or anything else with which the reader interacts. Rather, Humor That Works contends to be an expert in training, facilitation, simplifying concepts, and using humor to be more productive, less stressed, and happier. The goal is for every reader to find one idea that will change the way they work. One idea that is new to them, or perhaps just a reminder of something they've learned before, that causes them to change the way they work for the better. That's it. Only one single idea. That's not so hard, is it?

4. Humor That Works can guarantee, with one hundred (100) percent certainty, and without reservation, hesitation, or regret, that there will be puns in this book. They will likely be puns that make you groan, boo, or otherwise roll your eyes. Humor That Works

makes no apologies for this and will continue to pun regardless of reader response. These puns are not for the reader, but for the amusement of the Humor That Works author. After all, the author wrote the book, so he should have some say as to what's included.

5. There may be additional things that need disclaiming, such as items regarding liability (we're not liable for stuff, ya know) and endorsement (things Humor That Works references aren't necessarily endorsements, unless they specifically say "I endorse this" and even then you have to determine the level of facetiousness employed). Also anything else we might have reasonably forgotten, such as telepathy, telekinesis, and/or use of the Force.

To continue, please select an option below.

AGREE   DISAGREE   AGREE TO DISAGREE

I

THE
WHAT
AND
WHY
OF
HUMOR

. . .

Conversations with the Editor, Part I

"Do you really have to start with why humor
is important?"

"Yes."

"But no one thinks humor is a bad thing."

"That's true, but most people think it's a nice-
to-have. But in order for people to be successful in
today's world, humor is a must-have."

"Really? A must-have? Like it's just as important as
leadership skills or being able to communicate?"

"Exactly."

"I don't know if I agree with that."

"That's why I have to start with why humor
is important."

1
Humanity's Desperate
Need for Humor

• • •

COULD SENSE AMY was still mad at me. Mostly because
she had just said, "I'm still mad at you." I may be an engineer, but even I can pick up on clues like that.

It was my junior year at the Ohio State University and my
second year as a resident advisor (RA). If you're not familiar
with the role of an RA, they're basically freshmen babysitters,
an intermediary between students having parental supervision
before college and the free-for-all that is life off-campus and
post-graduation. In short, RAs try to make sure students don't
do too much damage to themselves or their GPAS.

Amy and I were co-RAs, together responsible for 46 freshmen living on the second floor of Smith Hall. The two of us
worked well as a team: I was good with the paperwork and Amy
was good with the humans.

Amy had suggested we host a dinner for our residents.
I assumed we would take them to the cafeteria and use our

15

meal plan—easy-peasy. But Amy wanted to *cook* for them. That seemed less efficient to me, but since Amy was in charge of sapiens-related matters, cooking it was. We decided to cook the simplest thing you can for a large group: spaghetti.

It's important to note that I am not a very good cook. The most advanced thing I can handle are Pop-Tarts. And I don't even put them in a toaster, I eat them raw. The night of, I decided I would just watch Amy and mimic what she did.

I watched as she took out a pot, filled it with water, put it on a burner and turned it on, let the water boil, and then put the spaghetti in. That seemed easy enough; I could do that. In fact, I could do it more efficiently.

I took out a pot, filled it with water, put it on a burner, immediately put the spaghetti in, and then turned the burner on to let the water boil... That's wrong. I still don't know *why* it's wrong, but in that moment, I knew it was wrong because Amy flipped out. "What are you doing??? You have to let the water boil first!" She rushed over and dumped everything out. "You... you just get out of the kitchen."

So I talked to the residents while Amy prepared everything: the spaghetti, the garlic bread, the salad, the grated cheese (which I felt like I could have at least handled that). But she did it all, and the entire floor enjoyed a delicious meal.

Amy and I were cleaning up afterward, and that's when she said, "I'm still mad at you."

"I'm sorry! I've never made spaghetti before."

"I'm mad because you always do this!"

Not realizing I should cut my losses, I replied, "Umm, how can I always do this if this is the first time we've cooked together?"

Amy rolled her eyes so hard it was audible. "I'm not talking about the spaghetti," she replied, about to drop knowledge on me. "I'm talking about how you always try to take shortcuts.

You always try to do the least amount of work possible. You do it with your schoolwork, you do it with your residents, and you do it with me."

Amy was right. I was treating my residents like a checklist: three minutes with this person, three minutes with that person, three minutes with Amy equals I'm an amazing RA. But that's not how relationships work. That's not how teams work. That's not how humans work. In my quest for ruthless efficiency, I was forgetting an important fact: we are not robots.

People versus Machines

There is a difference between being efficient and being effective. You can be efficient with things like computers: you don't need to motivate a computer to work, you don't have to convince it to turn on, it doesn't need a cup of coffee before it starts in the morning. But you can't be efficient with people. Because people have "emotions" and "feelings," and they get "sick" and "tired," and they have to "eat" and "sleep." Instead, you have to be effective.

Yet, we label people as resources. Just as computers or raw materials are resources, we say humans are a resource. And over time, we start to forget that the person on the other side of an email, phone call, or conference desk is a fellow human being with all the complexity of a human life and human emotions. And maybe, just maybe, the reason our coworker hasn't replied to that email yet isn't because they secretly hate us, but because they're dealing with a sick kid at home or are overwhelmed with work. We blame others for not working with the efficiency of a machine regardless of circumstance: "If only Jerry in accounting would respond to my 26-page email I sent 12 seconds ago."

We even do it with ourselves. When things aren't going well, we beat ourselves up about it. If we're behind in work, we think, "If only I were more disciplined," or "If only I were faster." And we justify our behavior by saying we're busy.

If you ask someone, "How are things?" the response is almost always, "Busy." Or maybe, "Crazy busy." Or, "Oh you know, busy busy busy." Everyone is busy.

Of course, not so busy that we can't watch four hours of television every day, spend another three hours on the internet, or waste at least twenty minutes trying to decide what to watch on Netflix before just turning on reruns of *The Office* again. But we are busy. Busier than ever, in fact.

The Evolution of Productivity

In the earliest days of humans, your only job was survival. You tried to live long enough to have children and maybe make a cool cave painting or two. Working was hunting, gathering, and getting lit (i.e., making fires, not getting drunk).

Then in 9500 BC, humans started farming and the agricultural revolution began. For the next 11,000 years, the majority of the work people did was grow crops. You planted, you tended, you harvested. Any notion of productivity was limited to how much food you could produce. There were no conversations about work/life balance and no employee surveys to determine your engagement. You worked so you could eat.

The meaning of productivity evolved in the mid-1700s with the Industrial Revolution: as food production increased and required fewer human hands, working people were freed up to do other jobs. This period of history was obsessed with efficiency: how do you produce more with less? Answer: machinery, like the cotton gin, and factory setups, like the mouse-run sweatshop from *An American Tail* starring Fievel Mousekewitz.

The Origin of Corporate Speak

Some of you may have already been familiar with the general history of work, but most people don't know that many of the corporate phrases we use today all came from the same meeting.*

In the mid-1950s, a big company had a business meeting with the theme "Do More with Less" that they held at a zoo to save money (and "provide a unique team-building environment"). During the last day of the three-day offsite, the project manager was giving a status update when an elephant walked into the room, getting in people's way, constantly muting and unmuting the conference line, and eating that one Danish that had been sitting on the table for two days.

The project manager tried to ignore the distraction and continue the presentation until finally someone piped up, "Hold on, can we please talk about the elephant in the room?" That set off a series of other complaints.

"Well, if we're going to talk about the elephant, can we please put the moose on the table?"

"Whoa, hold those horses. I think we first need to get all of these ducks in a row."

"Great, now you've let the cat out of the bag. People, we're all getting distracted by red herrings. We need to let sleeping dogs lie."

Finally, the project manager agreed. "That's right. We could argue about all of this until the cows come home. Let's end this wild goose chase and move them all to the parking lot so we can continue."

---

* This is (probably) not true.

By 1791, Benjamin Franklin wrote one of the earliest known to-do lists. Had he been born a few hundred years earlier, it would have simply read, "Wake up. Find food. Don't die." But instead, it listed things like "read," "music," and a generic task of "work," which I'm assuming included "put key on a kite" and "pose for picture for future use on a $100 bill." Life, for some, had evolved from survival to self-efficacy.

As the decades rolled on, the political and economic landscapes led to greater and greater need for productivity: in the United States, entry into World War I, the Roaring Twenties, the Great Depression, World War II, and the desire to read the entire Lord of the Rings trilogy meant producing more using less. Efficiency and productivity then entered the American home with a greater reliance on canned goods, TV dinners, and microwave ovens. It would be years before these microwaves would add preset buttons for what manufacturers must assume are the staples of an American diet—pizza, popcorn, and baked potatoes—but the transition had begun.

From there, technology exploded in a push for increased productivity: the PC, world wide web, and my personal favorite, spreadsheets, made employees more productive. Personal digital assistants (PDAs) in the 1990s forecasted the rise of mobile work, which came fully mainstream with the iPhone in 2007 and the various smartphones, smartwatches, and (what I'm assuming exist) smartcufflinks we have today.

Why the history lesson? Because the quest for greater and greater efficiency neglects the human capacity for work. And up until the last 40 or so years, an obsession with efficiency had little downside. During the industrial age, factory lines made optimizing resources a top priority. The repetitive nature of work meant shaving half a second off an action could lead to millions of dollars in time and cost savings.

But we now live in the information age, and the way we work has changed. Efficiency still matters, but so does effectiveness. Many of us are now knowledge workers, and knowing is half the battle (thanks, GI Joe). The other half is action. In today's work environment, motivation and engagement have become core factors of productivity. People's emotions can now dramatically affect their ability to deliver results.

Yet we still treat people like machines, and it's impacting not just our work but also our lives.

The Cost of the Way We Work

As an engineer, I love numbers. They make sense. My favorite number? All of them. My favorite, favorite number? 8. It's a perfect closed loop, an infinity sign standing up, a zero with a belt on, and it's part of the greatest kids joke of all time: Why was six afraid of seven? Because seven eight nine. Or the Yoda version: Why was five afraid of seven? Because six, seven eight.

Numbers can be beautiful: 2,479,991,040 is the average life expectancy in minutes. They can be nostalgic: 07734 is "hello" on an upside-down calculator. They can be nerdy: 37579.2 is my birthday in stardate format. And they can be illuminating: they can help quantify the world around us so we can understand our realities, challenges, and opportunities. Which also means they can be scary. Don't believe me? Consider how many buildings skip floor 13. But there are even scarier numbers than that.

In today's world, 83 percent of Americans are stressed out at work, 55 percent are unsatisfied with their jobs, and 47 percent struggle to stay happy. (Of course, it's even worse in Disney World where, statistically, only one out of seven dwarfs is Happy...)

It all leads to the US economy losing nearly one trillion dollars every year:

- $500 billion in lost productivity from disengaged employees.
- $300 billion in productivity and healthcare costs from stressed-out workers.
- $11 billion in productivity and replacement costs due to employee turnover.

That's $811 billion lost every year, bigger than the GDP of 160 countries, including Switzerland, Argentina, and the Federated States of Micronesia. If you were to stretch that $811 billion out in ones around the world, most of the money would get wet. And it would wrap around the Earth more than 1,300 times.

The problem is that it's hard to contextualize a number like $811 billion. It's like saying there are 10 quintillion insects on Earth. That's a 10 with 18 zeros after it. That just sounds like a lot. But if you translate that number to the fact that there are 300 pounds of insects per pound of human on this planet? That's just gross.

So, let's do some math.

If there are 154 million working Americans, and studies show 70 percent of the workforce is disengaged, that's 107.8 million people not engaged at work (versus the number who got engaged at work, which is probably lower because the workplace seems like an unlikely place to propose). If that costs the US economy $500 billion in lost productivity, that's $4,638 in lost productivity per disengaged employee, every year.

But that's not the only impact.

$$154,000,000 \times 0.7 = 107,800,000$$

$$\frac{\$500,000,000,000}{107,800,000} = \$4,638$$

Consider stress and turnover: 97 million Americans report high stress at work, and employers pay $68 billion in direct stress-related costs every year. This is because stressed employees are more likely to get sick, have increased blood pressure, and spend more money on hair dye because of all of their grays. In fact, the type A personality so many of us identify as was originally an assessment of who was at higher risk for heart disease. So, when you boast that you're type A, you're saying, "Hey, I might die sooner!" Doing the math, every high-stressed employee costs their company an extra $701, just in increased healthcare costs.

$$\frac{\$68,000,000,000}{97,000,000} = \$701$$

When you throw in lost productivity, absenteeism, and crying in the bathroom, the American Psychological Association estimates the cost of each stressed employee at $7,500. Think of all the stressed-out people you know and imagine having an extra $7,500 for each one of them; that's a lot of money.

And when it comes to turnover, the average cost to replace an employee is estimated to be between 20 and 120 percent of that person's salary. If we take the average wage in the United States at roughly $44,000 and assume the lowest cost to replace them, that's $8,800 per employee who quits.

That's just to get a new employee up to speed, saying nothing about the impact someone's departure has on group dynamics, project lead times, or intramural softball teams.

$$\$44,000 \times 0.2 = \$8,800$$

But there's one last set of numbers that is truly scary. The examples so far have all focused on the impact to the company, and some of you may be moved by that. Maybe you're the CEO or company founder, a senior leader, or someone who really believes in the mission of your organization. Those numbers are important. But what about the impact on you, the individual reading this book?

The first truly scary number: 90,000.

That's the number of hours the average person works in their lifetime. 90,000 hours. That is 10.2 years of 24/7, 365. That is more time than it would take to watch everything on Netflix. That is a lot of time.

But again, that's hard to imagine, so here's the second truly scary number: 33.6.

No matter who you are or what you do, you get 168 hours in a week. If you average seven hours of sleep each night, that's 49 hours spent sleeping, leaving 119 hours left awake. If you work an average of 40 hours a week, and I'm sure many of you are way above that, that's 33.6 percent of your awake adult life spent at work. One-third of your waking life!

If 70 percent of people are disengaged in something they do 33.6 percent of the time, something is wrong. The current way of working isn't actually working.

If we want to fix these numbers, we have to change the way we work. And to do that, it's not about changing what we do, it's about changing *how* we do it.

The What of Work

If you look at the basic components of work—what we do for 40-plus hours a week—there are only five things. No matter your role, function, background, history, or job title, your work boils down to some percentage of the following five skills.

Execution

Can you complete tasks? Can you update a spreadsheet, sustain productivity throughout the day, or professionally shave an alpaca? This is the starting point for most entry-level jobs (execution, that is, not alpaca shaving). Execution involves productivity, discipline, motivation, and stress management. If you can't execute, you can't work.

Thinking

Can you create a course of action? Can you strategically plan a project, brainstorm new ideas, or figure out how many engineers it takes to screw in a lightbulb?[2] This is what many of us start learning at university, and this skill carries over to the highest echelons of work: strategic thinking, planning, problem-solving, creativity, and innovation. If you can't think, you can't advance.

---

2   The answer is one. Engineers are efficient and not always funny.

Communication

Can you clearly articulate and understand ideas? Can you send an email that gets a response, explain an idea so people understand it, or translate messages written entirely in emojis? This is the foundation of being able to work with other people. Communication includes speaking, listening, reading, writing, and understanding nonverbal cues. If you can't communicate, you can't influence.

Connection

Can you build relationships with fellow humans? Can you find common ground with a coworker, build rapport with a client, or engage in small talk with people standing next to you in an elevator? This is required to get things done in any type of group setting. Connection involves empathy, bonding, networking, and shared experiences. If you can't connect, you can't survive.

Leadership

Can you influence people toward a goal? Can you create a compelling vision that people will follow, generate momentum in a team, or be the first to have some cake while everyone else is standing around being polite? This is the primary difference between the average employee and one with high potential. Leadership includes setting a direction, inspiring others, providing guidance, and driving change. If you can't lead, you can't create lasting impact.

That's it: the What of Work. If you work, you execute, think, communicate, connect, and lead. That's true whether you're a senior executive, firefighter, or dog trainer. I know because we at Humor That Works have worked with all of them (the dog trainers even called me a "good boy"). But beyond these five skills, there is one last skill that is often missing that amplifies the other five; one last skill that doesn't focus on what you do but on how you do it.

The Missing Skill

After my spaghetti fiasco with Amy, I started re-evaluating how I approached being an RA. I wondered what else I was doing efficiently that wasn't all that effective. I tried connecting more with my residents and I didn't shortcut my conversations with Amy, even when that meant talking for 20 minutes about a dog she *might* get.

And I changed how I planned programs for the floor. Prior to spaghetti-gate, I copied from other RAs, delivering your standard "bring in a guidance counselor to help residents pick a major," "diversity is important because I said so," and "don't drink and drive because it's bad" type of programs. They presented valuable information but were terribly boring. So boring that I often hated being at my own events. And apparently my residents did too, because they rarely attended. But after the floor dinner, I decided to stop with the shortcuts. If I was going to go through the hassle of putting on a program, I decided I should at least have fun doing it, even if that meant doing a little more work. That way, even if no one showed up, I would still have a good time.

So I created more interesting events. We had *Halo* tournaments, root beer Olympics, and dodgeball. We still covered the same educational topics; we just did it in a more interesting way. The events were fun and engaging, and I thoroughly enjoyed them. Apparently my residents did too, because they almost always attended.

I didn't realize it at the time, but I had stumbled on an important lesson and had started using the missing skill of work. As it turns out, people are more willing to do what they find fun, and that's what people are missing: humor that works.

2
Why Choose Humor

• • •

I T WAS LATE on a Monday afternoon when my coworker Sarah pulled me aside. I had just wrapped up my weekly status meeting at Procter & Gamble for Project Awesomization, a yearlong project revitalizing the retail sales portal for the $350-million Prestige division.

Surprised by our impromptu meeting, I asked Sarah what was up.

She replied, "I just wanted to thank you."

I had no idea what she was thanking me for, so naturally I responded, "It's about time... Why are you thanking me?"

"For this project; it's been fun."

I was ecstatic. "Finally! Someone else who appreciates the joy of Bayesian probability and predictive analytics. You know, analyzing sales data really gets a bad rap."

She cut me off. "What are you talking about? No, not the project itself. I'm talking about the way you're managing it.

Before I started on Project Awesomization, I was stressed out and thinking about quitting. I hated Monday mornings and even dreaded Sundays, because I would start thinking about work. But then I joined your team and it's been different; it's been fun. I mean, the project is called Project Awesomization, and you teach us improv exercises, and we took a quiz to see which Star Wars character we are. And I realized that no one told you to use humor: you just decided to. So, thank you."

I was touched, because Sarah, a.k.a. Ewok, was right.[3] No one ever told me to use humor, but no one ever stopped me either.

I've found ways to have fun in every job I've ever had. When I pushed carts at a grocery store, I would invent games like "kick the rock" to pass the time with my friends on shift. When I worked in a factory one summer, I came up with nerdy rap lyrics in my head to make the day go by faster. When I did data entry as an intern, I listened to upbeat music and typed to the beat.

Even at P&G as an "adult," I found all sorts of ways to make the job more fun for myself and others. Ewok, like so many other people, never thought she could use humor at work. I always assumed I could. And that's how I've found success.

The Benefits of Humor

When I tell people that employees who use humor at work are more productive, less stressed, and happier, they are admittedly a bit skeptical.

Don't get me wrong, no one really thinks of humor as a bad thing. Is there anyone who hates to laugh? Anyone who hates feeling joy in their body? No. Most people think of it as a nice-to-have: "Sure, I'd love to enjoy my work more, but if not, what can I do?"

---

3   Technically Sarah got Wicket W. Warrick, but she didn't like that name so we called her Ewok instead.

But humor is a must-have. In today's overworked, under-appreciated, stress-filled, sleep-deprived world, humor is a necessity. Don't take my word for it: consider the research that has been done at universities like Harvard and Stanford, case studies at companies like Google and Southwest, and stories shared in publications like the *Wall Street Journal* and *this book*.

Using humor in your message can get people to stop—hammertime—and pay attention. Humor also makes your message more memorable and improves long-term memory retention. Simple things like mnemonics stay with us long after we first learn them—I haven't played an instrument in years, but I still remember that that Every Good Boy Deserves Fudge.

Humor also increases our ability to solve problems by warming up the brain. In fact, I can help you get some neurons going right now with a pun:

I eat my cereal at the end of the kitchen counter because I like to experience Life on the edge.

Just by reading a simple joke, our brain starts making connections and, in the process, releases serotonin, a neurotransmitter that improves focus and increases overall brainpower. And if you laughed at that joke, then congratulations, you also just burned half of a calorie... which is 15 percent of a single M&M. That may not seem like much, but if you laugh for 10 to 15 minutes, you'll burn as many calories as five minutes of aerobic exercise, 10 minutes of dancing, or 15 minutes of milking a cow.

If you do that every day for a year, you could lose up to four pounds. If you do that for a lifetime, you'll reduce anxiety, relieve frustration, increase resiliency, lower blood pressure, boost your immune system, and become one of those fun old people, not a curmudgeonly one who yells, "Get off my lawn!"

And if you're more productive and less stressed, you can see how you might be paid more. A study in the *Harvard Business*

Review found that executives who used humor were promoted faster and earned more money. While money may not buy happiness, relationships might. People with three close friends at work were 96 percent more likely to be satisfied with their lives. Not just satisfied with their work, but satisfied with their lives. And how do you make close friends? Money.

Just kidding. By using humor.

Because humor connects people. It builds trust, defuses tension, and creates a positive shared experience that brings people closer together. And this is just the beginning.

30 Benefits You Get from Humor at Work

1. Improves productivity.
2. Reduces stress.
3. Prevents burnout.
4. Provides motivation.
5. Increases size of paycheck.
6. Boosts overall brainpower.
7. Improves decision-making.
8. Increases the acceptance of ideas.
9. Triggers new connections.
10. Enhances problem-solving skills.
11. Gets people to listen.
12. Improves memory retention.
13. Boosts persuasion.
14. Assists in learning.
15. Increases likability.
16. Connects us with others.
17. Fosters rapport.
18. Reduces status differentials.
19. Builds trust.
20. Encourages collaboration.
21. Enhances leadership skills.
22. Defuses conflict.
23. Creates more opportunities.
24. Builds credibility.
25. Improves ratings.
26. Increases ability to cope.
27. Strengthens the immune system.
28. Relaxes muscles.
29. Burns calories.
30. Increases happiness.

I didn't make any of these up: they're all backed by research, case studies, and real-world examples.[4] Yes, even #27—laughter is the best medicine (after actual medicine).

Now imagine when an entire team or organization incorporates humor as part of the workplace culture. You have employees who enjoy what they do and actually want to show up to work. You see teams that work well together and have each other's backs. You build habits of happiness and gratitude within the entire organization. And people become more present, positive, productive, and ultimately more profitable.

10 Benefits Your Organization Gets from Humor at Work

1. Creates a more positive work culture.
2. Improves morale.
3. Strengthens loyalty.
4. Decreases turnover.
5. Increases job satisfaction.
6. Boosts engagement.
7. Reduces absenteeism.
8. Builds team cohesion.
9. Enhances group productivity.
10. Raises profit.

I'm still not making these up. As the title of John Morreall's book so aptly proclaims, *Humor Works*. It's no wonder that in a survey of 1,000 executives, 84 percent of respondents felt that workers with a sense of humor do a better job. A separate survey of more than 700 CEOs found that 98 percent of them preferred job candidates with a sense of humor. It does make you wonder about the 2 percent who don't want humor, doesn't it?

"Hey, do you want to raise profits while also improving morale?"

"No thanks, I hate money and happiness."

My guess is that either those CEOs are secretly T-1000 robots sent from the future to destroy fun—or they've experienced the dark side of humor.

---

4   Seriously, check out the Sources section.

The Dangers of Humor

. . . .

It would be easy to focus only on the positives of humor. After all, this is a book encouraging humor in the workplace; telling you the good is part of the strategy to convince you to start using it. But it would be wrong to not mention the dangers of humor, like how it's wrong to stand on the left side of escalators. (Look, if you want to use those 20 seconds to rest, great. Just do it on the right side, so those of us who want to rise more efficiently can.) Bob Mankoff, former cartoon editor at the *New Yorker*, says humor can "unite and divide, teach and taunt, attract and repel."

Given this dichotomy, I would love to create an entire Jedi analogy around the light and dark side of humor, but that would imply that the good and bad create balance. I even hesitate saying humor is a double-edged sword (or lightsaber) because that also suggests two equal sides of good and bad.

Instead, I'll say humor is like a screwdriver (*Doctor Who* fans, feel free to imagine a sonic screwdriver). A screwdriver is an incredibly effective tool that often involves a twist and, when used in the right context, can help you construct and deconstruct any number of objects. But, in order to get the benefits, you have to use it correctly. If you try to use a Phillips head screwdriver on one of those screws that looks like a star, it won't fit. And though a screwdriver is meant to be a tool, you *could* try to stab someone with it.

Non-metaphorical translation: humor is a fantastic tool when used appropriately. When it's not, it can have serious consequences.

Danger #1: It Can Distract People

Distraction can sometimes be a good thing. If you're stressed out at work and near the point of burnout, taking a break to recharge can be valuable (and might even be a strategy talked about later in this book). But distraction can also create disaster. As Dr. Jim Lyttle shared in his paper on the judicious use of humor in the workplace, "While [humor] may seem harmless enough on a personal level, tomfoolery can lead workers to ignore quality or safety standards." If you're working in a factory and are too focused on your music, you could accidentally run into a wall or get hit by a forklift. Or if you're working on a presentation, you might go down a rabbit hole of finding the perfect dog picture to include rather than focusing on building the rest of the content. Because humor is fun, it can keep people from focusing on the right things.

One of the first humor workshops I delivered at P&G was on using humor for innovation. The feedback after the event was that it was too fun. Too fun? That's a thing? But to one person it was. "I had a lot of fun, but I don't see how it's going to help me do my job better." I had failed to make a clear connection between the exercises and their impact—how making up words and defining them uses the same creative muscles as coming up with innovative solutions. I've since learned how to better connect the fun with its function.

Some people also use humor as an alternative to getting anything done. Humor doesn't replace work. If your boss says, "Hey, do you have those TPS reports?" You can't respond with a joke and move on. You actually have to do the TPS reports, Peter. (Shout-out to *Office Space*, still one of the best worst cinematic workplaces and the inspiration for red staplers everywhere.)

Humor can also be used to strategically create inaction. That's why court jesters existed in a monarchy. A court jester was granted permission to poke fun at the court and point out its absurdities so that the onlookers would laugh, tension would be released, and the threat of revolt would diminish. This still holds true today when, for example, joking about an inequality replaces actually rectifying it.

Danger #2: It Can Divide People

Humor has this incredible ability to bring people closer. When we laugh or smile together, we create a human-to-human connection. But it can also divide us.

"Although humor unifies, it also can divide by creating in- and out-groups and accentuating power differences," says John C. Meyer, associate professor of speech communication at the University of Southern Mississippi. If you're not in on the joke, humor doesn't create connection, it destroys it. The shared laughter of the in-group says, "We're cool with each other but not with you," like just about everything the Plastics do in *Mean Girls*. It can feel isolating and is a clear signal that "you can't sit with us."

It's also why the dreaded "mandatory fun" can do more harm than good. Trust falls have become synonymous with team-building awfulness because they attempt to manufacture connection. For the people who just want to go home or would rather be focused on the work piling up on their desk, the experience that is supposed to bring people closer is only driving them further away.

Danger #3: It Can Disparage People

At its best, humor is a positive force for good. At its worst, it's a tool used to suppress ideas, destroy self-esteem, and make people feel terrible.

"Disparagement humor can foster discrimination against targeted groups," explains Dr. Thomas Ford, a researcher of prejudice, discrimination, and humor at Western Carolina

University. "For prejudiced people, the belief that 'a disparaging joke is just a joke' trivializes the mistreatment of historically oppressed social groups."

If you work in an environment where people are constantly made fun of or ridiculed, it changes your behavior—you're less likely to share new ideas or to be yourself out of fear of repercussions. If you're often the butt of a joke, it can damage your self-esteem. This is even true if you're the one making the joke, which is why self-deprecating humor should be used with caution. This negative effect is compounded when leaders use aggressive humor. One study found that when leaders used disparaging humor, their employees were more likely to engage in bad behavior and were less likely to be engaged in their work.

Humor is a tool, and just like any tool, it can be used to create or destroy. Like anything with an associated risk, it's important to understand its potential dangers, so they can be mitigated rather than ignored completely. I've dropped my phone on my toe at least 17 times in my life, but that doesn't mean I'm going to give it up and start sending messenger pigeons (how would I send a gif?). Humor carries some risk, but the pros far outweigh the cons.

The Opportunity in Humor

In the first chapter, I talked about how numbers can be scary and how quantifying some of the realities of the way we work is depressing. But numbers can also be uplifting. After all, they aren't math problems, they're math opportunities.

What's the true dollar value of the benefits we've shared so far? Let's return to the math.

If 70 percent of the workforce is disengaged, with each disengaged employee costing their company an average of

$4,638, that means an organization of 100 people could be losing up to $324,660 every year.

$$100 \times 0.7 \times \$4,638 = \$324,660$$

That $324k is not only what's lost but also the opportunity. Let's say you implement a humor program for your organization. You bring in a humor engineer—one who loves puns and goes by Drew because it's more efficient—and you're able to re-engage half of those disengaged employees; you would gain $162k for the year. If you could re-engage three-quarters of them, that's $243k. All of them gets you the full $324k.

The same can be done for stress—$701 in direct savings for each employee you teach how to effectively manage their stress—and turnover, which gives you at least $8,800 for each employee you retain.

There's also opportunity in an area we didn't cover before: productivity. The average yearly output of a US employee, averaged across all business sectors, is valued at $102,996. For many of you, it's going to be higher. But taking that average, if you were to increase a single employee's productivity by 0.1 percent—the equivalent of two hours over the course of an entire year—you've gained $103.

$$\$102,996 \times 0.001 = \$103$$

Now, $103 isn't a lot of money, but it is five times the cost of this book. You multiply that by an organization of 500 people and it's now an increase of $51,500. Or let's say your program makes them an entire 1 percent more productive—1.6 hours a month—that's more than $1,000 per employee, or $500,000 for 500 people.

What's the point of these very conservative estimates? First, math is fun. (In fact, I recently started counting calories; I'm not dieting, I just love counting.) Second, it's to show that humor isn't just a nice-to-have, it's not just something to do because "humans shouldn't hate their job" or "maybe we should actually like that thing we spend 33.6 percent of our time doing." No, humor is a must-have, and it's a strategic business decision not enough people are making.

HUMOR = $$$

Why People Don't Use Humor

"What do you do if you don't think your boss would approve of humor?"

That was the question from one of the 50 students who had come to hear me speak at Prague College in the Czech Republic. I started to respond when he added, "Keep in mind, I'm a German guy working for a German company with a German boss."

I laughed. "Let me ask you this," I replied. "Does your boss appreciate efficiency?"

"Yes."

"And what about effectiveness?"

"Yes."

"Do you think he'd be open to something that would make you more efficient, more effective, or possibly both?"

"Yes."

"Great, so if you had proof that humor makes you more effective, say, in the form of 30 benefits of humor, backed by research, case studies, and real-world examples that you could share with him, do you think he'd be more open to the idea of humor?"

"Yes."

"Perfect, I'm happy to share those with you. Let me ask you one more question: have you ever tried using humor?"

There was a pause. "No."

I've had similar conversations in programs all around the world, though usually not so efficiently. Which leads to an important question: if humor is so valuable, why don't people use it more?

It's something I wanted to better understand, so we ran a study through *Humor That Works*. We surveyed more than 700 people and asked a few questions, including:

How important is humor in the workplace?

Roughly 70 percent of respondents said humor is important or very important. Less than 2 percent said it was not important at all, and 28 percent said "maybe?" The most important question we asked was:

What is preventing you from using humor at work?

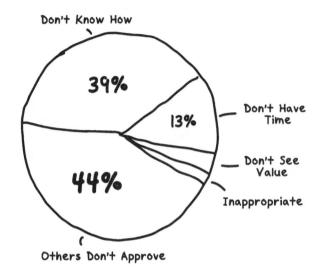

Don't Know How

39%

13% — Don't Have Time

— Don't See Value

Inappropriate

44%

Others Don't Approve

"I Don't Think My Boss or Coworkers Would Approve"

The number one reason respondents gave for why they don't use humor is that they don't think their boss or coworkers would approve (44 percent). If you fall into this camp and you work for yourself, it's time to sit down in front of a mirror and have a one-on-one with yourself.

For the non-self-employed, this fear is understandable. When humor isn't the norm in a workplace, it can feel unwelcome. The sad thing is, in many cases, people never even try using humor at work. They just assume that boring is the way it has to be, not knowing that their coworkers are clamoring for fun as much as they are. A study of more than 2,500 employees found that 81 percent of them said a fun workplace would make them more productive. Even more surprising is that 55 percent said they would take less pay to have more fun. I'm not suggesting you trade moolah for hoopla—after all, why not have more money and more funny?—but the stats speak to how desperately it's desired. Plus, we already talked about the 98 percent of CEOs who prefer it.

That's not to say that there aren't cases where humor has been actively discouraged. There are some workplaces and some managers who aren't yet hip to humor. In those cases, it's often a lack of education (show them the research!) or a result of poorly used humor in the past. But even if you feel like you're in an environment where humor is frowned upon, no one can stop you from finding ways to make your *own* work more fun (just check out chapter 5: Humor and Execution).

"I Don't Know How"

The second reason people said they don't use humor is that they don't know how (39 percent). This is usually split between people who don't think they can be funny (they can—anyone can learn to be funnier) or they don't know how to do it appropriately (this can also be learned, even by people who love "that's what she said" jokes). Both of these things are covered in this book, so just keep reading.

"I Don't Have Time"

The third reason respondents said they don't use humor is that they don't have time (13 percent). They don't have time to make things more fun. That's crazy, right? It's like wanting to take a time-management course but not having the time to do it. Lest we forget the two scariest numbers of work: 90,000 and 33.6 percent. The truth is that it all comes down to a decision, one you make every day.

Humor Survey Says ...

We asked some other questions on the survey that weren't directly related to using humor at work but that I found interesting. For starters, we asked, "What one thing would make your workplace happier?" Responses included:

- "More work flexibility."
- "More money."
- "Less blah blah blahing."

The occupations of respondents varied dramatically, including doctors, nurses, managers, marketers, military personnel, engineers, teachers, students, one cartoon editor, and someone who described their job as "open people up & see what's the happs."

Of respondents, 45 percent worked in business, 16 percent in education, 12 percent in healthcare, and 10 percent were students; 17 percent chose not to reveal their occupations, so they were obviously spies. Of those in business, 29 percent were in management, 17 percent in administrative, 10 percent in IT, 9 percent in sales, 9 percent in marketing, 9 percent in finance, 7 percent in HR, and 10 percent didn't share (corporate spies!).

Blue was the winner for favorite color at 18 percent. It was followed by green (16 percent), purple (12 percent), and red (11 percent). Only 6 percent of respondents shared my favorite color, orange.

Some of the songs that respondents were listening to included:

- ABBA's "Dancing Queen"
- Toby Keith's "Red Solo Cup"
- 2Pac's "Changes"

The variety of responses is fascinating but, even more important, shows the diversity of the people who appreciate humor in the workplace (and ABBA).

Humor Is a Choice

. . . .

A few months after my interaction with Sarah, I pulled her aside after a meeting.

"Hey, Ewok, I just wanted to thank you."

"R-drew, D-drew," she replied. "That's so sweet of you. What did I do?"

"A little while ago you thanked me for making the project fun, and it really stuck with me. I think I've realized that's what I want to do for a living. I want to teach people how they can enjoy their work more so they can do it better."

She smiled, "I think you'd be great at it. I say go for it."

And then she added something so simple and yet so profound: "After all, you are responsible for your own happiness."

You are responsible for your own happiness. It's true. It is not up to your coworkers or your boss to make sure you enjoy what you do. Fun is not a guaranteed benefit that a company provides. Happiness is not for others to generate for you.

Hopefully the people around you don't make you unhappy, and there are things they can do to help, but it's not up to them. You are responsible for your own happiness.

If you don't like a task you have to do, if you dislike a coworker you have to work with, if you dread going to work on Monday morning—whatever it may be that you don't like about your work, you are responsible for it. It's up to you to either change it or change the way you think about it. If you are going to work 90,000 hours in your lifetime, you might as well enjoy them.

3
Defining Humor That Works

• • •

I WAS HANGING OUT with some friends when I felt my phone buzz. I checked my messages and was surprised to find a text message from my grandmother. I was surprised because my grandmother had never texted me before. She was 78 years old at the time, had grown up without a phone, and suddenly had an iPhone.

That first message was adorable. It read, "Dear Andrew, Trying Out Texting. Love, Your Grandma."

Awww, I thought, *she thinks it's a letter.* So I sent a response back: "Hey Grandma, it's a text, you don't have to include all that."

Her response: "Dear Andrew, OK. Love, Your Grandma."

My favorite part is that it's always "Love, *Your* Grandma." Like if she said, "Love, Grandma," I'd be confused. "Dear Andrew, Have a good time in Singapore! Love, Grandma," I'd be like, "'Love Grandma'? Whose grandma?"

But over the years, *my* grandma has gotten better at texting. She'll use the occasional emoji, she can send pictures, and she even understands some of the texting acronyms. Just... not all of them.

A few years after her first text, I went to Switzerland to speak at a couple of events. I came back and sent her a text: "Hey Grandma, just got back from Switzerland."

Her response was, "Dear Andrew, Switzerland? WTF."

I was shocked. What had become of my dear old grandmother? So, I called Grandma up and asked, "Grandma, what do you think WTF means?"

She responded, "Well, someone at bridge told me it means 'Wow, that's fun.'"

All I could do was laugh and say, "That is exactly what it means," because I'm not explaining what it actually means to my grandmother.

But it turns out that the secret to being more productive, less stressed, and happier in the workplace is to think like my grandmother: to look at the world and think, "Wow, that's fun." Because humor is a mindset, a way of seeing the world.

The Definition of Humor

What comes to mind when you think of the word "humor"?

Many people think of laughter, comedy, or jokes. Maybe a sense of joy or fun, or ice cream (shout-out to the Good Humor man). But what does it really mean?

The dictionary definition of the word humor is (drumroll please):

a comic, absurd, or incongruous quality causing amusement.

So comedy is included. But it's broader than that; it's something that is a little silly, or a little different, that brings joy. It could be a joke you tell, an applied improv activity you do, or a simple use of the word "razzmatazz."

It's like in grade school when you learned that all lions are cats but not all cats are lions. That's the relationship between humor and comedy: all comedy is humor but not all humor is comedy.

To demonstrate, here's a diagram my buddy Venn made:

The joke "a leader of an orchestra was recently hit by lightning, proving he was, after all, a good conductor" is humorous, but so is a smile. Humor is anything that causes amusement—anything that "helps pass time pleasantly" or "entertains or diverts in an enjoyable or cheerful manner." But what classifies something as humor?

As it turns out, no one really knows for sure. Psychologists, philosophers, linguists, and that guy at the bar who's had one too many ("Oh you think that's funny? I'll show you funny!") have theories and ideas, but none are universally accepted.

Experts can't even agree on how to classify the act of classifying humor.

Some classify humor by the *what*: what is causing the humor? Is it the release of tension (relief theory), getting joy from the misfortunes of others (superiority theory), or the recognition of something surprising (incongruity theory)? Others classify humor by structure (script-based semantic theory) or by process and timing (computational-neural theory). Some suggest it's a combination of two or more theories (benign violation theory), and that guy at the bar is probably passed out by now.

Personally, I've found that trying to understand how to classify humor is harder than learning how to create it. Luckily, we don't have to know exactly how humor works to be adept at using it. I have no ideas how the zeros and ones in my pocket go to outer space and end up in your pocket, but that doesn't stop me from using my cell phone.

For our intents and purposes (I won't say "all intents and purposes" because other people have valid reasons to classify differently), I'll define humor that works as:

a way of working that is different, effective, and fun.

That's it. Despite the way many people think about the word humor, we're going to use this broader definition. Different because, as Jay Baer says in his book *Talk Triggers*, "same is lame." Effective because we're focused on what works. And fun because when we enjoy what we do, we do it better.

Humor That Doesn't Work

Mike looked around the office as people sat working away in their open space environment, some bouncing on those giant yoga balls you really want to kick whenever you see them, others at standing desks who never remained standing for very long. What he didn't see was anyone playing at the ping-pong tables, sitting in the beanbag chairs, or getting beer from the keg on tap.

"No one plays ping-pong, except maybe once or twice a month. The sound of the ping-pong balls going back and forth is incredibly annoying to anyone not playing. We tried getting the balls that don't make much sound, but they suck.

"You'll rarely see anyone sitting in the beanbag chair area. It can be nice for a quick conversation when visitors come in, but they aren't very practical for work meetings. It's hard to find a comfortable position to type notes in, and have you ever tried to get out of a beanbag chair gracefully? It's impossible."

As for the tap? "Oh yeah, that one actually gets used quite a bit. We have Beer:30 on Friday afternoons where people will grab a beer and chit chat if they'd like. I do wonder if bug reports are higher on Mondays, though . . ."

Mike's story echoes what I hear from a lot of people who work at startups. There are plenty of symbols representing the startup world—the ping-pong table being perhaps the most ubiquitous—to suggest you're at a "fun" company and that humor is part of the culture. None of these things are bad, but they don't guarantee a fun workplace.

"The worst," Mike shared with me, "is the unlimited vacation policy. In theory, it sounds amazing. 'Take vacation whenever you want'—who wouldn't like that? The problem is that there's also no minimum that you have to take. And the unwritten rule here is that if you have time to take vacation, you're not important to the success of the company. And since no one else does it, unlimited basically means zero."

Humor isn't a set of toys or HR policies, although my mom, who works in HR, likes to say, "You can't spell humor without HR.

Otherwise it'd just be 'umo.'" Humor is a way of behaving, a way of interacting with each other, and a way of working. And it's going to be different for every person.

Cooking Up Humor

We all know that I'm a terrible cook (I can't even do spaghetti!). Does that mean I starve? No. Because there is more than one way to obtain food. I can hire someone else to cook (eat at a restaurant), use what's already been made (frozen dinners from the store), follow a set of instructions (read a recipe), or do it all on my own (just throw in some ingredients).

Humor is the same. You can hire someone else to do it (bring in a humor engineer), use what's already been made (share appropriate humor from other people), follow a set of instructions (read Part II of this book), or do it all on your own (find your own ways to have fun).

Following that metaphor, think of this book as a cookbook (punny apron not included). Following the instructions won't automatically make you a gourmet humorist, but it will help you cook up some fun. And like a cookbook, it can't tell you what to do in every situation that could ever arise, but it will help you get started.

Perhaps the most important part of this analogy is with respect to individual preference. Everyone's taste buds are different. My taste buds like milkshakes and dislike beets. And yet there are people who eat beets presumably because their taste buds love dirt. That's because different people have different tastes (both in food and humor).

Generally, a person who has used inappropriate humor at work and a person who has cooked an unpopular dish have made the same mistake: satisfying their personal tastes rather than considering the people on the receiving end.

Inappropriate Humor

In my 10-plus years of working on humor in the workplace, I've never heard of anyone getting fired because of a bad joke. People have been fired because of an inappropriate joke but not a bad joke.

In fact, a study conducted at Harvard and Wharton found, "Bad jokes—as long as they are appropriate—won't harm your social standing or affect how competent people think you are. They may even increase how confident you seem." That's why I have no qualms about the number of puns in this book.

This is also great news because people are often worried about what will happen if a joke falls flat or if they try to use humor and no one laughs. Telling an appropriate joke, whether it lands or not, has very little risk. And if it's successful? "A well-executed appropriate joke makes you seem more confident, more competent, and higher status."

But telling an inappropriate joke is different. That same study found, "Inappropriate–joke tellers were perceived as less competent and lower status than serious responders, even when the joke was funny."

The general thesis for the impact of a joke is:

Appropriate and Successful

Appropriate but Unsuccessful

Inappropriate but Successful

Inappropriate and Unsuccessful

So what's the difference between a bad joke and an inappropriate one? A bad joke is something like, "I once had to miss class because of hypothermia: I was too cool for school." That's a bad joke (but I still love it).

An inappropriate joke talks about an inappropriate topic, has an inappropriate target, or comes at an inappropriate time.

Inappropriate Topic

A few years ago, two people were conversing at a tech conference when they started making sexual jokes about dongles and forking (if you're not familiar, both are legitimate terms in tech, but you can also see how they could be used as innuendo). Another attendee at the conference overheard them, tweeted a picture of the two calling them out for making sexual jokes, and, 48 hours later, one of the people making the jokes and the person who tweeted about it were both fired from their respective companies.

This situation, as is often true of cases involving humor, is not black and white. Humor sometimes introduces a gray area of appropriate and inappropriate. If the two people joking were being sexually explicit about a specific person, that would clearly be inappropriate. If the two were making wordplay about dogs ("When it's raining cats and dogs, be careful not to step in a poodle"), that would clearly be appropriate (and adorable).

But when wordplay includes innuendo, it becomes less clear. The reaction from the community at large after the story broke showed the divide: some people said the jokes were in poor taste and inappropriate at the conference, others said they were harmless jokes in a private conversation, and a few asked, "Seriously, why is it called a dongle?" The aftermath of the incident was that two people lost their jobs, one because of the jokes and another because of how the matter was handled.

The important thing to take away is why the humor was deemed inappropriate; in this case, it's because of the topic. Just because something is "just a joke," it doesn't mean it's okay for it to be talked about in the workplace. If you wouldn't normally touch the subject in a regular work conversation, then it's not something you should talk about with humor.

Yes, stand-up comedians talk about all matter of topics in their stand-up sets. But your goal in using humor at work isn't to be a comedian, it's to get better results. That means knowing what is and isn't appropriate to talk about.

Inappropriate Target

Back in 2011, three employees of the Iowa Civil Rights Commission were fired over the emails they were sending about their coworkers. The emails were insulting in nature and included nicknames, like Psycho, Teen Wolf, and Homeless McGee. When confronted, one of the employees claimed the emails were just banter, a little harmless water-cooler talk between them. Their employer disagreed.

Humor has the powerful ability to unite or divide. In the case above, coworkers were using mean-spirited nicknames and comments as a way to create an in-group and out-group. Like we covered in chapter 2's Dangers of Humor, humor that takes aim at someone else can quickly go from fun and light-hearted to exclusionary and polarizing, which is inappropriate for any place, not just work.

There are certainly times when other people frustrate us, and maybe even deserve to be called not-so-polite names, but that doesn't fix the problem or improve the situation, and it's certainly not humor that works.

Inappropriate Time

Immediately after devastating tsunamis hit Japan back in 2011, Gilbert Gottfried decided it was time to make jokes about the situation. The jokes weren't funny to begin with, but they were also clearly too soon. Some moments are inherently serious, and trying to lighten them with humor can not only come across badly, it can also make a difficult situation even worse. Firing someone is not the time to bust out a *Frozen* parody: "I've got to let you goooo, let you goooooo, I can't pay you back anymore."

That's not to say humor can't be valuable during times of stress or crisis. Look at the headlines from the satirical newspaper *The Onion* 16 days after 9/11.

Hijackers Surprised to Find Selves in Hell

Not Knowing What Else to Do, Woman Bakes American-
   Flag Cake

God Angrily Clarifies "Don't Kill" Rule

The United States was in mourning and in need of catharsis, and *The Onion* provided it. They weren't flippant and they didn't make light of the tragedy; instead, they found a way to relieve some of the tension so many people were feeling.

It's suggested that comedy equals tragedy plus time. And there is some truth to that: time allows us to process stressful situations, and we can often look back at what seemed to be a nerve-wracking experience and laugh about it (like that time I dyed my hair platinum blond as if I was trying out for a boy band).

But that timing is important, and that's why "too soon" is part of our language around comedy. The difference between *The Onion* headlines and Gottfried's jokes is one of intent, meaning, and execution.

So how do you avoid inappropriate humor? It's helpful to know what your options are.

The Four Styles of Humor
. . . .

Psychologist Rod A. Martin has been studying humor for the past 30-plus years. In the 1990s, he started exploring whether the positive benefits of humor on health and well-being might be more related to *how* people use humor, as opposed to the degree in which they *have* a sense of humor. This disconnect between being funny and being happy led Martin, along with Patricia Puhlik-Doris, to create the Humor Styles Questionnaire, which identifies four styles of humor across two primary dimensions: positive/negative and social/self. Those four styles are:

- **Affiliative:** Amusing others as a way to facilitate relationships.
- **Self-enhancing:** Finding amusement in life's hardships.
- **Self-defeating:** Saying funny things at one's own expense.
- **Aggressive:** Disparaging others to manipulate them.

To better understand how to use appropriate humor in the workplace, let's look at each one in more detail.

Affiliative Humor
Affiliative is the best type of humor to use at work. It helps build and establish relationships with others and is positive—meaning there's no real target receiving the brunt of the punchline. It is welcoming of others and helps to make the office a better place. It's basically Ellen DeGeneres and Mister Rogers.

Affiliative humor in the workplace includes things like team-building activities, where they may not be laugh-out-loud funny, but after the activity, the group is stronger. Keeping in mind our broader definition of humor, some examples of affiliative humor include:

- Starting a lunch bunch to get to know coworkers better.
- Taking an improv workshop with your peers.
- Doing community service as an entire organization.

If you're ever in doubt as to what type of humor to use, stick with affiliative.

Self-Enhancing Humor

Self-enhancing humor is a close second to affiliative humor for its usefulness at work. It's all about finding amusement in the various challenges and struggles that exist in the corporate world. As Kurt Vonnegut said, "Laughter and tears are both responses to frustration and exhaustion. I myself prefer to laugh, since there is less cleaning up to do afterward."

If you're on a project or in a role you don't enjoy, self-enhancing humor can make it more bearable or just make your day-to-day work more fun. This is how I started using humor in the workplace. I remember being in a meeting that was so boring, I would have rather been stuck on an elevator forced to make small talk for an hour. The biggest issue, of course, was that I was the one leading the meeting. And I realized that if I was bored while talking, my team had to be bored while listening. That's when I decided to start making things more fun, not only for my team but also for my own sanity.

By finding ways to look at things from a different, more humorous angle, you can improve your overall enjoyment and satisfaction no matter what workplace you're in.

Some examples of self-enhancing humor include:

- Using pictures instead of words in a presentation.
- Listening to music while doing repetitive tasks like data entry.
- Solving a Rubik's cube while listening in on a conference call.

One of the best things about many forms of self-enhancing humor is that no one can prevent you from doing them. So even if you work in an environment where humor isn't welcome, you can apply it to your own role for your own benefit.

Meetings and Meetings

Self-enhancing humor is vital to surviving the workplace. There are deadlines, budget cuts, leadership changes... and that's just in trying to decide what to do for lunch. But there are also mountains of emails, a web of conference calls, and far too many coworkers who feel like they can text you whenever they want. On top of all that, there are meetings.

You have team meetings, group meetings, org meetings, and one-on-one meetings. There are meetings with your manager, meetings with your peers, meeting with your direct reports, and meetings with yourself because no one else showed up.

You have lunch-time meetings, brunch-time meetings, and it's getting down to crunch-time meetings. Meetings over coffee, meetings over drinks, meetings over dinner, and meetings over body shots because happy hour has gotten way out of control.

There are daily meetings, weekly meetings, monthly meetings, quarterly meetings, and yearly meetings. Plus bi-weekly meetings, semi-monthly meetings, and meetings to explain that bi-weekly and semi-monthly basically mean the same thing.

There are meetings you go to for the content. Meetings you go to for the people. Meetings you go to for the food. And of course, my favorite, meetings you go to to prepare for other meetings. Because we all know that no work actually gets done in meetings: it's all in the smaller meetings you had leading up to the bigger meeting. Which, of course, will only lead to more meetings.

But my biggest beef with meetings is that, despite the name, they're rarely about me. But if you're going to spend so much time sitting in meetings, you might as well make them fun.

Self-Defeating Humor

Self-defeating humor is a form of negative humor, where the target is you. It involves poking fun at yourself as a way to show humility or gain approval or acceptance.

Self-defeating humor can be very effective when you are at the top of the hierarchy. If you're the CEO, the leader of a project, or the one with authority, self-defeating humor can show your audience/direct reports/peers that you have a sense of humor and you don't take yourself too seriously.

It can also help ease tension and get people on your side. When I'm talking with students who might perceive me as being in some type of leadership position—by function of being brought in as a speaker—I'll make fun of how skinny I am (I was born 8.3 pounds and stayed that way until I was 15 years old) or talk about my laziness (if I know I'm going to wear a sport coat, I only iron the front of my shirt).

Some examples of self-defeating humor include:

- Calling out an obvious personal characteristic.
- Referencing your clumsiness if you trip on the stairs.
- Sharing an embarrassing story with a direct report.

Self-defeating humor does have its time and place, but it can also be detrimental. Using it when in a low status position or using it too much, regardless of your position, can turn it from a confident way of showing self-awareness to looking as if you are seeking pity. It also requires a lot of confidence to use and, if executed poorly, can be seen as insensitive.

For these reasons, self-defeating humor should be used only in moderation and in reference to something unrelated to your primary job responsibilities (e.g., your love for '90s boy-band music, not your "ineptitude" at "running" a "company").

Aggressive Humor

Aggressive humor is the most negative of the four types of humor. It has someone or something else as a target, and it's used to attack the credibility, beliefs, or even existence of that target. George Carlin was a master of this. ("Think of how stupid the average person is, and realize half of them are stupider than that.")

Aggressive humor has a place in the world—things like satire and sarcasm can be effective means of pointing out the absurdities of situations, and it can get people to think in a new way. It can also serve as catharsis for those in oppressive circumstances.

The problem with aggressive humor in the workplace is that, while it can help people blow off steam, it does so at someone's expense and it rarely creates positive change. If you work for a terrible boss, it might relieve stress to do insulting impressions of them behind their back, but it doesn't make things better. Instead, it's better to use self-enhancing humor as a way of improving the situation.

Some examples of appropriate aggressive humor include:

- ...

Only a Sith deals in absolutes, so I won't say that aggressive humor should *never* be used, but there's no consistent way to use it strategically. Stick with the other forms of humor.

The Newspaper Rule

The easiest way to check whether or not your humor is appropriate for the workplace is to think of the newspaper rule: would you be comfortable with whatever you said or did showing up on the front page of your hometown newspaper? Would you want your boss, your coworkers, your mom, or your parakeet to read about it?

If yes, you're probably okay. If you're hesitant—"not sure I want my mom to read that..."—then it's probably best to avoid. If you're thinking, *But my mom has a dark sense of humor and curses like a sailor*, then consider what my mom would think instead (as a reminder: she works in HR).

Humor Is a Mindset

Recently, my WTF grandma elevated her game from texting to Facebook. She loves seeing pictures of all her grandkids, staying connected to her friends, and commenting on all of my puns and one-liners. The problem is that I can't tell if she's the nicest, most sincere grandmother in the world... or if she is secretly trolling me.

A while back, I posted, *I'm trying to decide if I should become an athlete or a criminal, so I made a list of pros and cons.*

My grandmother's response was one word: "Funny." I'm not sure if she actually thought it was funny or if she was being sarcastic.

A few weeks later, I posted, *I think a cozy bar that serves figs would make for a plum date spot.*

My grandmother's response: "Ha, ha." There's something about that comma that makes me think she didn't really mean that.

And then finally, a short while after that, I posted, *Converting the numbers 51, 6, and 500 to Roman numerals makes me LIVID.*

My grandmother's response was, "Hey this one is actually good."

Trolled by my own grandmother.

The key to developing a humor habit is understanding that humor is a mindset. It's not about cracking jokes or telling the funniest stories (though that could be included): it's a way of seeing the world. It's a way of working that is different, effective, and fun.

It doesn't matter your age, your background, or your level of humor training, anyone can choose to have a humor mindset. All you have to do is be more like my grandmother and think WTF: "Wow, that's fun."

4

The Skill of
Humor

● ● ●

THE MAN STANDING across from me looked familiar. We were both waiting to do our AV checks for the internal TEDx event for P&G in Switzerland, and I wasn't sure if he and I had met before or if he just had "one of those faces" (a.k.a. an introvert's worst nightmare, where complete strangers assume they know you). So I decided to skip the awkwardness of "nice to meet you" versus "good to see you again" and jumped straight into standard speaker small talk: "What are you speaking on today?"

"I'm talking about some of the conservation efforts we're working on in South Africa," was the man's reply.

"That's cool. What are you conserving?" I asked.

"Most of my work is with lions."

"Wait . . ." It clicked why this man looked so familiar to me. "Are you the lion whisperer?!?"

Kevin blushed ever so slightly. "I used to hate that nickname, but yeah, I'm Kevin Richardson."

If you don't recognize the name Kevin Richardson, a.k.a. the Lion Whisperer, you've probably seen one of his videos on YouTube. If you've seen a lion hugging a dude, or a lioness on a hunt with a GoPro on its back, or some guy taking a nap on a lion's stomach, that's Kevin. He lives in South Africa, he raises lions from when they're cubs, and they treat him as one of the pride. He's basically Rafiki from *The Lion King*.

"That's incredible," I replied. "I can't wait to hear you speak."

"Thanks, I'm a bit nervous. What are you speaking on?"

"Me? Humor in the workplace."

"Humor in the workplace?"

"Yeah, I'm an engineer, but I started doing improv and stand-up comedy and realized it was helping me get better results."

"Wow, you do stand-up?" He paused. "I could never do that, it's too scary."

It took me a second to process. I looked around to see if I was the only one who had just heard what he'd said. I was.

"But . . . but you live with lions!"

Kevin smiled. "Lions are easy; people are hard."

I was shocked. I know people are afraid of public speaking, but suggesting that talking into a microphone is somehow scarier than *living with lions*?

But that's the perception: that humor is somehow innate. As if it's encoded in our DNA. That people are "naturally funny," and if you're not one of the lucky few, well then good luck ever pulling it off. But the truth is far different; the truth is that humor can be learned.

Learning Humor

I've done more than 1,000 shows as a stand-up comedian, improviser, storyteller, and spoken word artist. I've spoken or performed in all 50 states, in 20-plus countries, and on one planet (Earth). But when I recently went to my high school reunion and old classmates found out I did comedy, they said, "But you're not funny."

Growing up, I was never the life of the party or the class clown. My senior year, I was voted teacher's pet. If you know your personality assessments, I'm a type A, blue square, conscientious INTJ with the sign of Aquarius. That means I'm an ambitious, stubborn introvert who likes long walks on the beach... by myself.

But we are not our personality assessments. We are defined by our actions. So, if we act as a humorist, we become a humorist, regardless of what Myers-Briggs or our high school classmates say. And that's where my third education at Ohio State came in.

In the spring of my sophomore year, a group of us were sitting around diligently ~~studying~~ playing *Halo: Combat Evolved*, when Nate, my best friend and *Halo* nemesis, said something that would change the rest of our lives: "We should start an improv group."

At the time, only a few of us had ever done improv (I was not one of them). Some had theater experience in high school (not me), and others seemed naturally funny (nope, not this guy). But six of us set out to create the 8th Floor Improv Comedy Group at the Ohio State University.

Admittedly, we were not very good. At least to start. We watched *Whose Line Is It Anyway?* and tried to repeat what we saw. What I didn't have in comedy skill, I made up for in comedy project management. We practiced three times a week, had a business meeting every Monday, and filmed all of our shows so we could watch like it was game tape.

And we got better. Over the course of two years, we went from performing in the basement of residence halls to performing twice a week at a theater near campus. The group, now celebrating more than 15 years, is still going.

I was not "funny" when we started college, and some might say I wasn't "funny" when we graduated. But I was hooked. And I learned improv, and later stand-up, the same way you learn anything: by practice and repetition.

Professional versus Personal Comedy

Professional comedy is hard. A comedian will perform a joke hundreds, maybe even thousands, of times to get the exact wording and timing right. Talk shows and sitcoms have staffs of 10 or more professionally trained writers who work together. Improvisers practice for hours every week to build rapport and group mind.

Fortunately, using humor in our own lives—and in the workplace—doesn't require the same rigor. That's not to say that it doesn't require practice, but it doesn't require obsession. Because the bar for comedy in a stand-up club is different than that in conversation.

In a club, the audience is expecting you to be funny. It creates a weird dynamic. If you tell someone you do comedy, they're skeptical. They think, *Okay, prove it.* Whereas if you're funny in conversation, it's a pleasant surprise.

The same is true in the workplace. No one is expecting your weekly status report to be hilarious. So, when you add a small joke at the end of it, or you replace your meeting summary with a haiku, or you simply smile as you walk through the office, it has a great impact.

And chances are there's some form of humor that you're already good at. Maybe you're great at telling stories, crafting them in a way that people hang on every word you say.

Or maybe you excel at delivering jokes with great timing on revealing the punchline. Maybe you're a good writer, a fantastic artist or musician, or really good at weird facial expressions.

There are things you already do well that can be used to deploy humor easily. That's the advantage in personal comedy: the bar is lower. The disadvantage is that the stakes tend to be higher. If a comedian tells a joke that doesn't go well, that's okay, they move on. If you share a joke in a meeting that doesn't go well, the consequences may be (or at least seem to be) more severe.

Luckily, we don't have to become professional comedians to learn comedy, but we can learn from the professionals.

The Skill of Humor

The skill of humor comes down to three things:

1. **Sense of Humor:** Can you experience humor?
2. **Ability to Humor:** Can you create humor?
3. **Agency with Humor:** Can you apply humor?

A sense of humor is something everyone has. The ability to humor is something anyone can learn. And agency with humor is something we can all benefit from. At the intersection of all three is a humor engineer, someone who can take what they find funny, turn it into humor, and apply it to achieve a goal. The key to changing how you work is in understanding all three.

Sense of Humor

The starting point for using and creating humor is a sense of humor, something every human has (even accountants... boom, score one for the engineers!). If you know someone who has never laughed, they probably just have a very specific sense of humor that you haven't been exposed to. Or they're a sentient robot from the future. But if they're human, they have humor.

A sense of humor is simply what makes you laugh, what makes you smile, or what makes you go, "Hmm, that's interesting." Your sense of humor is defined by your point of view.

Think about your favorite stand-up comedian. Eddie Izzard has a certain way of seeing the world, which is different than Ali Wong, which is different than Dave Chappelle, John Mulaney, or the Marvelous Mrs. Maisel. Each comedian has their own perspective and they use that perspective—a.k.a. what they find interesting—to create humor.

Compare these different takes on life:

- **"Life is pleasant.** Death is peaceful. It's the transition that's troublesome." Isaac Asimov
- **"We've had some fun tonight**... considering we're all gonna die someday." Steve Martin
- **"Life is about balance.** The good and the bad. The highs and the lows. The pina and the colada." Ellen DeGeneres

These one-liners all talk about the ups and downs of life; the difference is in their points of view.

Understanding and exploring your sense of humor is the key to finding humor in everyday life. The best way to start to refine your point of view is to simply take note (physically or mentally) of what piques your curiosity. Any time you're out in the world and think, *Hmm, that's interesting*, explore it further and form an opinion about it. It's not that funny things happen to funny people: funny people see the world in a funny way.

Truth in Comedy

Admittedly as I researched this section for humorous perspectives on life, I got sucked into a bit of a rabbit hole of one-liners. But research has found that when you enjoy humor, you're better able to deploy it.

So, rather than hoard the jokes myself (and waste all of that research time), here are some of my favorite one-liners about work, life, and everything in between.

- "I always arrive late at the office, but I make up for it by leaving early." Charles Lamb
- "I always wanted to be somebody, but I see now I should have been more specific." Lily Tomlin
- "Clothes make the man. Naked people have little or no influence on society." Mark Twain
- "Laziness is nothing more than the habit of resting before you get tired." Jules Renard
- "There is nothing better than a friend, unless it is a friend with chocolate." Linda Grayson
- "Honesty may be the best policy, but it's important to remember that apparently, by elimination, dishonesty is the second-best policy." George Carlin
- "Stay true to yourself. Never follow someone else's path unless you're in the woods and you're lost and you see a path. By all means, you should follow that." Ellen DeGeneres
- "I never met anybody who said when they were a kid, I wanna grow up and be a critic." Richard Pryor
- "My way of joking is to tell the truth. It's the funniest joke in the world." George Bernard Shaw

Ability to Humor

The ability to humor is simply being able to take something that you find amusing or funny and deliver it in a way that other people understand and enjoy. This is not a requirement for using humor in the workplace, but it is the key to "being funny" and is something that can be learned (like singing, dancing, or how to fold a fitted sheet).

It starts with exploring and heightening your sense of humor, something we can learn from improv. Improvisers at UCB, Second City, and ComedySportz accept and build, explore and heighten, find the interesting thing, and say, "If this is true, what else is true?"

In short, improvisers say *yes and*.

Yes and is the fundamental mindset of improvisation. It simply means looking at the current situation and building from it. It's also the easiest way to get better at conversational humor. When someone shares an idea while you're chatting with them, find a way to *yes and* it. It doesn't mean that you agree with the idea; it just means, "YES I heard what you said and accept that you offered it, AND here's how I'm going to build on that."

It's positive, it's inclusive, and it creates momentum in the conversation. You can also use a *yes and* mindset to take the kernel of an idea and build it into an entire story.

Eddie Izzard's bit on the Death Star cafeteria follows a kind of logic:

If, in Star Wars, the Death Star exists...
And if people live on the Death Star...
It must be true that there is a cafeteria on the Death Star...
So, it could be true that Darth Vader has visited that cafeteria.

And from that comes a hilarious five-minute bit about Darth Vader visiting the cafeteria on the Death Star.[5]

---

5   If you haven't seen the bit, check it out at gethumor.org/izzard.

Once you have the premise (from your sense of humor) and you've started to explore the idea (*yes and*), you can put it into a structure that will resonate with people. This is part of what comedians mean by "delivery."

The most common structure is a traditional joke: setup and punchline (setup: "a man asked if I wanted some free fish"; punchline: "I asked, 'What's the catch?'"). But stories are also a structure, as are associations, visuals, and more. These structures are simply a vehicle for sharing your sense of humor and a more refined way of *yes and*-ing it.

Delivery also involves using your humor with confidence. This comes from practice and repetition. You can take an improv class, try stand-up, or simply start working humor into more everyday situations (e.g., casual conversations, social media posts, group texts with your friends). The more you practice, perform, and repeat, the better you'll get at making people laugh or smile.

Agency of Humor

The final component of successfully using humor in the workplace is learning how to leverage your sense of humor and the ability to humor to achieve specific results. This is the true value of humor: not that it's fun, but that it's effective.

The interesting thing about your agency of humor is that you don't have to be the creator of humor to use it. David Nihill, ranked as one of the best public speaking coaches by *Forbes*, says, "One of the quickest ways to be funny is to use already proven images and videos. Let the content be the punchline."

Even if you don't think you're funny (though you can learn to be), or you aren't ready to try out any material of your own, you can be a shepherd of humor. You can take things you find funny (sense) and share it with others for specific goals (agency). You can use humorous quotations to make a point for you, attach memes to your email, or share a funny TEDX talk with your team. Just be sure to give proper credit and don't violate any copyright laws; there's nothing funny about a lawsuit (unless it's an actual suit made of printed-out laws).

The agency of humor is all about getting better results, and it happens by using one of the most important concepts in this book: the Humor MAP.

The Humor MAP

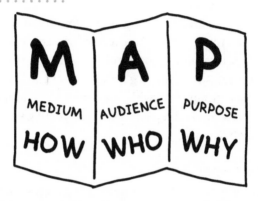

The Humor MAP is the easiest way to determine what type of humor to use, regardless of organization size, industry, or location. It also helps you choose the right humor for different cultures, different work contexts, and different times of day (my math jokes don't go over as well at 8 a.m. when people's coffee has yet to kick in).

It will serve as your guide. It will give you direction on where you need to go, help you avoid hazards, and make you legend-ary (and that's it for the map puns).

The MAP stands for:

- **Medium:** How are you going to execute the humor? Is it an image, video, text, or done live? Will it be in an email, document, meeting, or presentation?

- **Audience:** Who is the recipient of the humor? How many people? What do they know? What do they need? What do they expect? What is your relationship to them?
- **Purpose:** Why are you using humor? To execute faster, think smarter, communicate better, connect closer, or lead further?

If you know these three things, you'll have a good idea of what type of humor to use to get the results you want.

Medium

The medium is all about the how. How is the humor going to be received by the audience? Will it be in a live presentation with a speaker, prerecorded on a video the audience watches on a monitor, or written on a sheet of paper for them to read?

Depending on the medium, different types of humor are more effective. One type of humor (e.g., music) may be perfect for one medium (aural) but terrible for others (visual). And some of you may be confused by my classification of music as humor. Remember, humor is anything that is comic, absurd, or incongruous that causes amusement. Music can be all three. Take the chorus from this song by Rihanna:

> Work, work, work, work, work, work
> You see me I be work, work, work, work, work, work

This song was number one in America for nine weeks; it was nominated for two Grammy Awards. It was not because of how its lyrics read on the page. But when you hear Rihanna sing it, that's a different story.

When thinking about your medium, think about how the humor will be experienced. In real-time conversation, it's easy to gauge a reaction, and your delivery can help show that you're being facetious. Emails and texts are more easily misconstrued. "I hate you" seems pretty bad. "I hate you!" seems even worse. "I hate you :)" seems flirty. That's why we're seeing a rise in the use of emoticons, emojis, and gif responses. And with all the emoji options now, my phone is capable of expressing more emotion than I am (I've never once stuck out my tongue, winked, and blushed at the same time).

Understanding your medium means asking: is there a visual component to the delivery so people can read body language, or an aural component so people can pick up on paralanguage such as pitch, volume, and intonation? Is it preplanned or off the cuff? Is it in an email, on a conference call, or in one-on-one conversation? All of these details affect how your message is perceived. Think about what humor will work best for the medium you will use.

Audience

The next component of the Humor MAP is the audience, which is all about the who. Who will be the recipient of your humor? What do they know? What do they expect? What do they need? Understanding this—what the audience knows/expects/needs—is vital for all communication, not only humor (had the kidnappers in the movie *Taken* known what Liam Neeson's character knew, the movie would have been called *Not Taken*).

You also want to be clear about what your relationship is to the audience. A joke that you make with a coworker you've known for 10 years may be very different than what you might say to a client you're meeting for the first time. Sometimes the only difference between humor that is affiliative versus aggressive is your relationship with a person. In my friend group in college, if you weren't being made fun of, it meant we didn't like you; groups can be weird like that.

If you want to use humor effectively, you have to know your audience. That is the only way you can choose the right type of humor to fulfill your purpose. Otherwise, you run the risk of boring, confusing, alienating, or upsetting them. Your audience dictates whether or not what you say is funny—if they enjoy it, it is; if they don't, it isn't. The focus has to be on them. As a result, speaking their language is vital. It's like the time I told an older woman in London that I liked her pants. I was unaware that in the UK, pants means underwear. I was wondering why she winked at me.

Understanding your audience is crucial to creating humor that works. Because when you get it right, it unlocks incredible doors. When I was on the *Same Side Selling* podcast with Ian Altman, talking about how to use humor in selling, Ian shared an example of a salesperson he knew who would start all of his cold calls with, "This is a cold call. If you'd like to hang up, now's a good time to do it." He said that the salesperson almost always got a laugh. Plenty of people still hung up on him, but many more stayed on a little longer to hear what he had to say, because he proved he understood his audience by being direct about what they may want to do.

Humor relies on doing something a little different. If you don't know what an audience knows and expects, you can't relate to them while also creating surprise. Do your research about the recipient of your humor to increase the chance it will be effective.

Purpose

The final component of the Humor MAP is also the most important because it's all about the why. Why are you using humor? Is it to increase productivity, expand learning, or develop creativity? Like a five-year-old, you want to understand why, why, why, why, why.

Without knowing why you're using humor, you're likely to miss the mark and turn people off in the process. If you want to use humor to help people better understand a concept, including an analogy they don't get won't help.

Pretend you're a fashion designer tasked with creating a certain outfit, but you don't know for what purpose. Rather than find out, you just start sewing and end up making an incredibly elegant evening gown. In fact, this gown becomes recognized as being the best gown in the entire world, nay, entire universe. You take it to your client and, despite its beauty, he is not happy, because, while you made an incredible dress for a formal event, he needed a swimsuit.

Is it a silly example? Definitely. But it's no sillier than using humor without understanding why you're using it.

Humor for the sake of humor is perfectly fine, as long as you are conscious that that is your purpose. The humor you decide to use should be aligned with the outcome you hope to achieve.

This is also how you avoid being seen as a jester or clown at work. When people see that your humor is directly connected to getting better results, they see its value. It's not that so-and-so is always cracking jokes, it's that so-and-so is great at getting people to pay attention or leads these really great meetings or really likes Star Wars.

With a clear objective for using humor, you increase the chance that you'll not only delight your audience but also achieve your goals.

Humor Is a Strategy

I smiled as Kevin Richardson stepped off-stage. He had crushed it. People were engaged in his message the entire time, captivated by his passion for his work, and enthralled by the videos he had shared. He even got a few laughs from his stories. How can you not enjoy footage of a giant lioness licking a grown man's face?

Whether he knew it or not, Kevin already had the skill of humor, just as everyone does. The missing skill in achieving success and happiness in the workplace comes down to just being a little more deliberate about it; it comes down to using humor as a strategy.

It starts with your sense of humor: what do you find amusing and interesting in the world? You build on that sense of humor with your ability to humor: taking those interesting ideas and packaging them in a way that other people can consume. And you use your ability to humor to develop agency with humor: using those ideas to achieve certain goals.

As a humor engineer, you build that skill of humor by taking note of the world around you, continually improving, and following your Humor MAP. Success and happiness come from being deliberate in what you're after and finding a fun way to get there. Part II of this book teaches you how to do that.

"

THE
HOW
OF
HUMOR

. . .

Conversations with the Editor, Part II

"Okay, fine. Humor is a must-have."

"I agree."

"But how do I actually use it? I have a general idea, but I want action steps."

"That comes next. We can use humor to level up each of the five skills of work. By understanding the best principles for each skill, then adding humor to them, we can go from good to great."

"Was that a subtle shout-out to James C. Collins, author of *Good to Great*?"

"It was."

"Is this also when I'll learn to be funnier?"

"Some of the strategies will help. But remember, humor is broader than comedy. And this book isn't about being funnier: it's about being effective-er."

"Effective-er isn't a word."

"But you know what I mean."

"Well, yes, but—"

"Which means my made-up word was . . ."

". . . Effective."

":)"

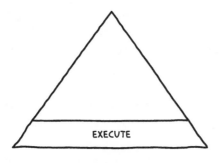

EXECUTE

5

Humor and Execution

. . .

THE SUMMER BEFORE my freshman year at Ohio State was best characterized by the aforementioned Rihanna song: work, work, work, work, work. Since I was putting myself through school, I worked two jobs to save up money to pay for things like room and board, books, and a compendium of video games.

The first job was in a factory that manufactured "luxury glass enclosures," a.k.a. shower doors. Monday to Friday, I worked from 6:30 a.m. to 3:30 p.m. (not as catchy as Dolly Parton's 9 to 5), helping fulfill orders by loading 50-pound shower doors onto pallets to be shipped to customers.

The work was repetitive, exhausting, and repetitive. I quickly realized I had to find a way to keep my mind busy—I feared

I would actually die from boredom (or a falling shower door). The options were limited. We weren't allowed to listen to music on headphones (a legit safety precaution), and there wasn't much time for conversation.

That left me with my thoughts and the small notebook I kept in my pocket. Given the circumstances, I decided to fill my mental time on the job by working on what I hoped would be my future career: hip-hop superstar.

As I walked around the warehouse, fulfilling orders, I would make rhymes in my head. My head would bob to the music in my mind as I created melodic messages with meaning and mirth. During breaks or in between orders, I would write down the rhymes in my notebook. Unsurprisingly, the songs were astonishingly terrible.[6] But those rhymes kept me engaged in my work and helped me pass the time until my second job.

After my shift at the factory ended, I would head to workplace number two: Meijer, a "modern supercenter"—like a cross between a Walmart and a Target. I was hired as a cashier, but I always asked to work outside pushing carts. As a cashier, you were beholden to the register; you had to stay there no matter how many customers came and went and no matter how fast you did your job. But outside with the carts, you controlled your own destiny.

As long as there were enough carts for the customers, you could bring them in however you wanted. I quickly learned that if you worked really hard for 30 minutes to get every single cart in the parking lot, it would take another 30 minutes for the parking lot to get full again ... And in that time, you could do whatever you wanted (I decided).

So I would schedule shifts with my friends, we'd bust our booties for 30 minutes, and then we'd relax. We'd go to the break room and watch *Jeopardy*, play Kick the Rock, or stop by

---

6   Need proof? Check out the SoundCloud page for Isaac Drewton: gethumor.org/drewton.

the kids' play area and catch part of the one movie played on a loop: the 1996 classic *Dunston Checks In*, starring Jason Alexander, Faye Dunaway, and an orangutan.

And that was my summer. Working 70-hour weeks, alternating between pulling shower doors and pushing carts, switching between making up rhymes and making up games. I didn't know it at the time, but these were the exact strategies anyone, in any role, can use to execute faster.

The What of Execution

The underlying skill of any job is the ability to execute. No matter your role or position, you have to actually be able to do things: send an email approving a merger, hold a firehose in a specific direction, or give a dog a treat for learning a new command.

It's pretty simple: if you can't do the job, you won't have a job. It makes sense then that incompetence—or lack of execution—is the number one reason why people are fired (ahead of lying, stealing, and calling your boss stupid on Twitter).

Execution is the link between goals and results; it's made up of the actions employees take every day to do their work. And it's the starting point for success because anyone can have an idea; the real value comes in how that idea is executed. That's why my uncle doesn't get any money from Apple even though he "totally came up with the idea for an iPod back in 1987."

As Brian Moran, author of *The 12-week Year*, explains, "The market only rewards those ideas that get implemented. Execution is the single greatest market differentiator. Great companies and successful individuals execute better than their competition." Or, as Yoda said, "Do or do not, there is no try."

Success in business is judged by execution, just as our opinions of others are judged by their actions. Despite how cool

Professor X is, he's fictional; humans aren't mind readers, so all we can judge others by is what they do. But paradoxically we judge ourselves by our intentions, by what we think.

Have you ever felt good about yourself because of something you thought? I remember being on the New York subway a few months after I moved there with P&G. It had been a long day, full of stressful meetings and dealing with someone who decided to do all of their conference calls, and a personal call with their doctor, on speakerphone; all I wanted to do was get home and veg out (which ironically never involves vegetables—mostly pizza and Netflix). An older woman got on the train, and she also looked a bit weary and worn from the day. And I thought to myself, *I should give her my seat. I'm a strong, spry young lad* (despite having just used the word "spry"), *and though I'm tired, I should stand up to let her sit.* I didn't do it, but I felt good about myself just for having thought it.

No one wakes up thinking, *You know what, I want to annoy people today. I want to lead a meeting so boring people want to cry. I want to send a thousand unnecessary emails. And I want to burn popcorn in the break room.* No one starts the day with those intentions, but they are all things that happen with frequency, often because of the same underlying reason. The key to executing well is what I learned from spaghetti-gate: understanding the difference between being efficient and being effective.

Efficient and Effective

Back in chapter 1, Humanity's Desperate Need for Humor, we covered society's obsession with efficiency and its impact on our ability to be effective (to the tune of $811 billion every year). That doesn't mean that efficiency is inherently bad; it just means that it's not the end-all, be-all (or be-all, end-all?) of how to execute. In fact, to execute faster, it's important to understand both efficiency and effectiveness.

Efficiency is about doing the least amount of work for the most amount of gain. Effectiveness is about getting the most amount of gain with the least amount of work. The two are similar, but the focus is different. Efficiency is focused on the work; effectiveness is focused on the result. Efficiency is completing a task; effectiveness is accomplishing a goal. Efficiency is running fast; effectiveness is winning the race.

The way we work can be both, neither, or one or the other.

The ideal is for work to be both, efficient and effective, like escalators and milkshakes. This is the primary goal in execution and makes engineers around the world happy. Examples include: putting whatever you need to remember the next day under your keys, the metric system, and closing a bag of chips without using a clip.[7]

Then there are things that are neither efficient nor effective, like those terrible customer service automated phone trees or the letter Q. In general, we try to avoid such things as much as possible, which is why I eschew fax machines, voicemail, and grocery shopping while hungry.

---

7   If you don't know the roll and fold method, put down your chips and watch this video: gethumor.org/roll.

There are things that seem efficient but aren't very effective. This includes multitasking, Crocs, and emails that skip the formalities ("Hello" and "Sincerely") and only make demands ("Send me the agenda!"). The problem is that these things are seductive (except maybe the Crocs) and the efficiency is alluring.

Take multitasking, for example: it sounds fantastic—getting two or more things done at the same time? It's like dual-wielding productivity—how efficient is that! The problem is that we, as humans, are single processor computers. We can only do one conscious activity at a time. Yes, we can walk and talk at the same time, but that's because walking doesn't require our deep attention (unless we've just gotten off a boat or a binger). But compare that to competitive sports.

When an Olympic sprinter is running a race, she isn't sending texts, checking email, or posting Insta stories about how well she's doing. She's concentrating on the task at hand: running as fast as possible. Yet when those of us in the corporate world take our proverbial starting positions (i.e., sit down to work), we have more distractions than ever before, and they affect our effectiveness.

Sure, William Shakespeare wrote 37 plays and invented more than 400 words, but he never got distracted by the internet where, at any time, he could be sucked down a rabbit hole of researching how many plays he had written or words he had invented. While the *never-ending* list of *countless* words he supposedly invented is *overblown* and *laughable*, it's *unquestionable* that this *useful* book on how *to humor employment* for *excitement* and better *engagement* would not exist if not for the *generous* number of words he made *accessible*.[8]

---

8 Yes, each italicized word is attributed to Shakespeare, and I was only in said rabbit hole for 138 minutes.

Shakespeare at the Office

Shakespeare certainly had a way with words (made-up or otherwise). And though he's best known as a playwright, it seems as if he knew the corporate world quite well.

- **When the Earnings Report Doesn't Look Great:**
  "There is nothing either good or bad, but thinking makes it so." *Hamlet*
- **When the Projector Goes Down and You're the First to Notice It Got Unplugged:**
  "Some are born great, some achieve greatness, and some have greatness thrust upon them." *Twelfth Night*
- **When People Ask Why You Only Schedule 15-Minute Meetings:**
  "Brevity is the soul of wit." *Hamlet*
- **When You Win the Office Fantasy Football League:**
  "Uneasy lies the head that wears a crown." *Henry IV, Part 2*
- **When Someone Asks a Dumb Question at a Meeting:**
  "The fool doth think he is wise, but the wise man knows himself to be a fool." *As You Like It*
- **When You're the First to Leave a Group Chat:**
  "Cowards die many times before their deaths; the valiant never taste of death but once." *Julius Caesar*
- **When You Put a Conference Call on Speakerphone:**
  "All the world's a stage, and all the men and women merely players." *As You Like It*
- **When You're Trying to Figure Out Which Row/Column to Put Data into in a Spreadsheet:**
  "2B, or not 2B: that is the question." *Hamlet*

In one study on multitasking, workers switched activities every three minutes and five seconds on average (interestingly, the same amount of time it takes to burn popcorn in the microwave). But when we multitask, we're actually single-tasking, switching back and forth between those tasks at a high rate. And every time we switch, there's a mental cost, either in focus or in ability.

A study by the Institute of Psychiatry at the University of London found that multitasking caused a greater decrease in IQ than smoking pot or losing a night of sleep. Not exactly a ringing endorsement for the effectiveness of something we all do every day (multitask, that is; I don't know your smoking or sleeping habits).

Finally, the last tasks are the ones that are inefficient but effective. These are things like eating healthy, expressing love, and sending a longer email that includes a warm introduction and ends, "Cheers! Best! Regards! Sincerely, yours truly, xoxo." And using humor. Taking the time to add humor to your work isn't always efficient, but when done properly, it is effective.

The problem is that this effectiveness isn't always obvious. The payoff for the longer email isn't immediate; it comes over time when you resolve issues faster because you have a better relationship with the recipient. Most inefficient but effective tasks are those related to the human experience, those that affect the emotion of our self or others.

In order to improve our execution, we have to better understand how we can be efficient and effective.

Efficient Execution

At first glance, EVE Online seems like any other MMORPG (massively multiplayer online role-playing game, for the non-video-game enthusiasts). You can create characters, customize your spaceship, and explore/fight your way across thousands of star systems with more than 500,000 other players.

But the game isn't just about living out your intergalactic fantasies. One of the options in your Neocom Menu—EVE-speak for "menu"—is something called Project Discovery. Accessing the option brings you to the avatar of Professor Michel Mayor, the real-life astrophysicist credited with discovering the first exoplanet in 1995 and member of the National Order of the Legion of Honour, the highest order of merit in France. The man is a knight, studies space, and is in a video game! #DreamsIdidntknowIhad

Your task in Project Discovery, should you choose to accept it, is to analyze a light curve graph that represents a star's luminosity over time. Using a set of specialized tools, you simply look for times when the star doesn't appear as bright. Once you've found a potential dip in brightness (a "transit event"), you submit your analysis. For your efforts, you are rewarded with Analysis Kredits, which allow you to level up and gain new apparel for your character, like the space version of those monthly subscription boxes for clothes. Oh, and you'll be helping scientists discover new exoplanets in real life.

That's right, your in-game actions can lead to real-world scientific discoveries as part of a joint effort between CCP Games (the developer of EVE Online), MMOS (software that takes real-world data and plugs it into games), and the University of Geneva (a university... in Geneva). Your results are sent to scientists at the university for further analysis as part of a process called transit photometry, a reliable but tedious process of detecting exoplanets by changes in the brightness of stars (and the name of my new synth band with our first single, "When You Study Stars, Your Future Is Bright.")

To date, the EVE Online community has helped discover 37 new exoplanets. Before that, more than 100,000 in-game pilots submitted more than 25 million classifications of human cells to the Human Protein Atlas, a scientific research program with the goal to explore the whole human proteome (it's like the genome but for proteins).

How did Project Discovery convince hundreds of thousands of people to do mundane tasks for free? By making it fun.

Enjoying What You Do

Think about the last time you were in a state of flow, a time when you were in the zone, you were focused on the task at hand, time flew by, and you were insanely productive. What allowed you to reach peak efficiency?

You most likely felt challenged by the task but confident in your ability to do it. You were optimistic about the results, and there's a good chance you enjoyed the work you were doing. And even if what you were doing was work, it probably felt like play. Because work and play are not opposites and they don't have to be mutually exclusive, despite what you might assume from the story of Jack, the dull boy. In fact, one of the best ways to increase efficiency is to combine the two in what's called gamification.

The mini-game in EVE Online is a clear example of playing work. By including a narrative and a sense of community (and competition), and by providing rewards such as custom decals and in-game currency, Project Discovery turned a mundane task into a rewarding experience.

But game theory can be applied outside of an actual video game, which you see in apps like MyFitnessPal (a food diary with a social component), Habitica (a task list that's structured like a role-playing game), and Zombies, Run! (a running app that helps you do interval training by intermittently telling you that zombies are attacking and you have to run to escape).

There are a few core components to gamification: providing rewards, encouraging competition, increasing the challenge, and adding a narrative. But perhaps the most important is also the simplest: making it fun.

A study on employee performance found that humor can increase the length of time you're willing to do a task without detracting from your ability to concentrate. Research by a team of economists at Warwick Business School suggests that there is a clear link between workers' happiness and their productivity.

Which makes sense: would you rather do something fun or not fun? It seems like an obvious choice, and yet so many people spend their time doing tasks they don't like. Not because they're anti-fun, they just don't realize there's a better way, like the people who still haven't learned how to close a bag of chips without a clip.

If you want to have more fun, you have two options. The first is what most people think of: do more of the things you already enjoy. And if you naturally find the work you do fun, people will tell you that you're incredibly fortunate, that you've found your calling, and that you're one of the lucky few.

But there's a second option: make more of the things you have to do fun. Pulling shower doors and pushing carts isn't the most exciting thing I've ever done, but I found ways to make the work more enjoyable. That's what I try to do with all my work. When my last book, *The United States of Laughter*, came out, I tried to have fun with it. A new book requires plenty of marketing, so when I sent out emails about its release, I included bad puns about publishing, such as:

- Why are millennials such great librarians? Because they're good with texts.
- Make sure you diligently follow all laws today. You should go buy the book. (Get it? Buy the book instead of by the book? No?)
- I'm trying to find a catapult so that I can truly celebrate this event with a book launch.

After hitting send on that last one, I thought, *I should actually do that.* I called around, found a group in Dayton, Ohio, that competes in pumpkin chucking challenges (shout-out to Team ETHOS), and I reached out. A few weeks later, I was strapping my book to a pumpkin and firing it out of a catapult—all so I could say I did a literal book launch.[9]

Remember: humor is a choice. Your work may not seem inherently fun, but that doesn't mean you can't find ways to make it so. And by choosing humor, you'll be choosing increased productivity, greater efficiency, and a more smile-worthy day. Which leads us to the first of 10 humor strategies for achieving success and happiness in the workplace, a way of increasing your efficiency at work.

Humor Strategy #1: Play Work

Playing your work is an easy way to start having more fun. Just like the developers of EVE Online, you can use game theory to turn mundane and boring tasks into a more enjoyable experience. It may not make you love your work, but it can keep you from hating it.

Adding a sense of play can be as simple as listening to your favorite music while you do data entry, reading emails in an accent in your head, or doodling visual notes while sitting in a meeting. You can also make it part of your larger strategy, like the Kiewit construction company, which turns part of their machine training into an Equipment Rodeo.

To play your work, take a task that you have to do and ask this simple question: "How do I make this more fun?" There are three primary ways to do that.

---

9   Want to see the video? Check it out at gethumor.org/booklaunch.

1. Turn the task into a game.

Think about how you can add game elements to the task. Brainstorm levels of completion for your work and then reward yourself when you reach new levels. Start a friendly competition with a coworker for who can complete tasks the fastest and take note of your best times. Or you could always work with a space knight to add exoplanet discovery into your MMORPG—whatever tickles your fancy.

2. Combine the task with something you love to do.

Look for ways to combine what you have to do with what you want to do. If you have to meet with someone and want to exercise, go for a walk and talk. Or if you're hungry, an eat and meet. If you have to commute to work and you want to learn all the words to "Bohemian Rhapsody," sing the song in the car. (Please don't do this if you take public transit. I don't care who you are: you're no Freddie Mercury.)

3. Complete the task with someone you like.

If all else fails, try to find someone to do the activity with. Even if the task itself isn't fun, the conversation around the task—or the commiserating after it's over—can make the experience more enjoyable. Call up a friend to catch up when you're stuck in traffic (hands-free, of course) or bring a close coworker with you to the networking event you have to attend. Personally, nothing seems quite as terrible if I can do it with someone I enjoy being around.

There are countless other ways to play your work: it's up to you to find the ones that work best for you. Using humor to execute with efficiency starts with the simple question: "How do I make this more fun?"

Effective Execution

The role of a banking and capital markets (BCM) auditor at a Big Four accounting firm is not an easy one. Throughout the year, they are responsible for enhancing corporate governance, providing financial reporting, and navigating regulatory complexity for some of the biggest names in banking (think JPMorgan Chase, not Big Bob's Banking Bodega).

The busiest time for the auditors is the eight weeks between the end of December and the end of February. In those two months, they have to complete a year's worth of auditing in order for their customers to hit their tax deadlines. During that time, it's common for the auditors to put in 60- to 80-hour weeks, spend weekends in the office, and see their coworkers more than their loved ones or beds.

Stress levels at that time are, as expected, very high. While there's nothing these firms can do to change the deadlines (aside from learning how to pause time or inventing a new month called Janubrary), they can help their employees relieve the stress of audit season.

Working together, Humor That Works and the human capital team for the BCM auditors at a Big Four firm developed a program to teach employees how to manage their stress using humor. The program was presented to more than 200 auditors before their busy season and was a resounding success, scoring a 4.9 out of 5.0 from the attendees and giving them a new outlook.

What did the program cover that helped auditors stay sane during the busiest time of year? The same thing anyone can learn to be more effective in the workplace: how to manage energy.

Stress Isn't a Bad Thing

As an engineer obsessed with efficiency, I've studied just about everything I can on productivity. I've read *Getting Things Done*, *The Effective Executive*, and *Smarter Faster Better*. I've done a deep dive on Parkinson's law, the Pareto principle, and the Pomodoro Technique. I've conducted a number of personal experiments to boost my own productivity, including tracking my time for an entire year, timing the duration and number of steps I take on my most frequent routes, and tracking my heart rate for more than 25 activities I do every day.[10]

In all of my research, I've come to the realization that it is very difficult to be productive if you are dead. Or if you feel like death, if you are stressed out, burned out, or worn out. It doesn't matter how much time you have if you have no energy or motivation to do anything with that time.

In chapter 1, Humanity's Desperate Need for Humor, we talked about the impact stress has on employees—to the tune of $701 in direct healthcare costs and an estimated $7,500 in absenteeism, disengagement, and hair dye. But stress isn't inherently a bad thing. In fact, it's absolutely necessary to becoming more efficient and effective in the workplace. As Dr. Heidi Hanna, author of *Stressaholic*, says, "A completely stress-free life would actually lead to atrophy and breakdown because we would lose the stimulation for growth."

Think about what happens when you exercise. Working out is the practice of stressing your muscles and body in the attempt to make them stronger. While you'll (hopefully) never have to run 26.2 consecutive miles, half a million people run a marathon every year for the purpose of pushing themselves physically and mentally (and because they're probably a little crazy).

---

10 To see the write-up of these personal experiments, check out gethumor.org/experiments.

The same is true for work. Whereas exercise stress strengthens our muscles and/or capacity to run, work stress strengthens our brain and capacity to get things done. The key to success in both is in how you manage your energy.

In *The Power of Full Engagement*, Jim Loehr and Tony Schwartz make the case that employees are essentially "corporate athletes," and we can learn how to reach peak performance at work by replicating what works for world-class sports athletes. They determined that the basic formula for high performance, whether it was on the field or in the boardroom, came down to how energy was expended (stress) and how it was renewed (recovery).

Which makes sense. We know that our muscles only grow when we provide them with fuel and give them time to rest. Personal growth at home and in the workplace requires the same thing: fuel and rest (and maybe a good book on personal development every now and then). So, the real problem isn't that we experience stress: it's how we handle it.

The key to being effective not just today or tomorrow but also next week, next month, next year, next decade, and (for those who believe in reincarnation) next lifetime is to manage the trials and tribulations of work and life well. This helps you be a better employee *and* a better friend, spouse, parent, and human. When you can manage the stress at home, you do better work. When you can manage the stress at work, you do better at life.

One way to do that is through humor. Humor is the anti-stress. A study on the effects of humor for coping found that people with a sense of humor reported less stress and anxiety than those with a low sense of humor, despite experiencing the same number of problems at work. Herbert M. Lefcourt, a clinical psychologist and distinguished professor emeritus at the University of Waterloo, says that "finding humor in stressful or potentially threatening situations can replace negative with positive affect, thereby giving people an increased ability to cope with negative states of affairs."

Which brings us to the second humor strategy: using humor to reboot stress.

Humor Strategy #2: Reboot Stress

Stress at work is inevitable. Suffering the negative effects of chronic stress is not. By consciously managing your stress levels, you can leverage stress for long-term growth and success. There are four effective ways to do that using humor.

1. Reject the things you hate.
The simplest but often hardest way to combat stress is to simply avoid it. Reject doing things that cause stress by either choosing not to do them or delegating them to someone else. For example, reading the news stresses me out: it's full of doom, gloom, and things that boomed. So, I stopped reading it first thing in the morning, replacing it with a crossword puzzle or jumping into creative work. I still want to be informed, so I've delegated the gathering of important news to other people, namely by reading Next Draft and The Hustle, two daily news curation services that share the news with a bit of humor.

Think about what you can stop doing by creating a to-don't list of the things on your to-do list that you no longer need to do. Be ruthless. If it's not something you have to do and it doesn't bring you joy (now or in the future), cut it or give it to someone else. Trust me, it's very cathartic.

2. Reframe the things you can't change.
Even after you reject the things you hate, stressful things you have to do—like commuting in rush hour—will remain. I, for

one, will be ecstatic when self-driving cars allow me to nap at 60 miles per hour. The next way to manage stress is to reframe how you think about it. Instead of lamenting over traffic, enjoy the additional time you have for an epic sing-along to *Hamilton*. This is what you're doing with the first humor strategy by playing your work: find ways to make the work you have to do more fun. It's a powerful use of self-enhancing humor by changing your perspective on the situation. If scientists can make transit photometry more fun, you can do it with emails, meetings, and status updates.

3. Relieve the stress you experience.
If you can't reject the stressful event, and you don't know how to reframe it more positively, you can at least relieve the stress it causes. No matter how diligently I plan, I will always experience travel delays, whether they're because of weather, mechanical issues, or ~~the pilot oversleeping~~ other mechanical issues. *Hamilton* is good, but it's not make-you-enjoy-sitting-in-an-airport-for-six-hours good.

The third way to manage stress is to be deliberate in how you de-stress after you be stressed. Exercising and meditating are great ways to do this, as is finding an excuse to laugh. Laughter counteracts the negative effects of chronic stress by increasing blood flow in the body, decreasing blood pressure, relaxing muscle tension, and reducing anxiety. If you had a long meeting, watch a funny YouTube video for a quick laugh. If you're working on a stressful project, take a break with a book. If it just hasn't been your day, your week, your month, or even your year, hang out with some Friends. The important thing is that when you've experienced something stressful, you do something to relieve it.

4. Recharge from the work at hand.

Even after employing the three previous methods, you may find you still have stress. That's life. But that's also why we have weekends and vacations. There are periods in my work—such as meeting this book deadline while traveling to five different continents in just over a month—that are plain-old stressful. The key is in actually taking a break to recombobulate every now and then.

The fourth way to handle stress is by recharging your human batteries. Studies have found that when an employee takes a vacation, they come back with increased feelings of productivity, ability to sleep, positive attitudes toward their jobs, and way too many Instagram selfies.

But taking a break shouldn't just be a weekly or monthly activity. It shouldn't even just be daily; there is strong evidence that points to the value of managing your stress at an hourly level. Research by chronobiologists (perhaps one of the coolest job titles) has found that most people's minds and bodies need recovery every 90 to 120 minutes. That's why planned breaks, like with the Pomodoro Technique, are so important.[11]

Rebooting stress is vital to being effective in the long-term, and a short break every now and then is a lot more efficient than the very long break that comes from being dead.

Executing with Humor

By the end of the summer before my freshman year of college, I had worked more than 800 hours pulling shower doors and pushing carts. I had saved up enough money to pay for room and board, books, and video games, and while I can't say that I loved either job, I had found ways to enjoy both.

---

11   For more on the Pomodoro Technique, check out gethumor.org/pomodoro.

Whether you work in a factory, at a grocery store, or in a corporate environment, being able to execute tasks is the foundation of any role. Successful execution comes down to efficiency and effectiveness—and recognizing the difference between the two.

To be efficient, play your work. Find ways to make it more fun so you do the work longer and actually look forward to going into the workplace. To be effective, reboot stress. Strategically recharge throughout the day to prevent chronic stress and burnout.

You decide how you do your work every single day. And even if your boss is staunchly anti-humor, they can't control how you think. They can't prevent you from reading emails in an accent in your head, listening to a comedy podcast on your way home from the office, or coming up with rap lyrics as you work. How you do your work is up to you, so why not use humor?

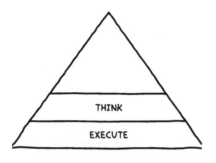

6

Humor and Thinking

• • •

IN 1983, APPLE released the Lisa, one of the first computers to offer a graphical user interface (GUI) and another example of technology sharing a name with a *Simpsons* character (like BART, the subway in San Francisco). To help navigate the screen, the computer came with a recently invented device for interacting with the machine: a single-button mouse.

While the Lisa was considered a flop (despite selling more than 100,000 units at $9,995 each), the mouse was a great success, with many of the original design elements still in use in mechanical mice today.

The group Steve Jobs hired to design the mouse for Apple, Hovey-Kelley, eventually became IDEO, the global design company responsible for hundreds of standard-setting designs, including the first laptop computer, the Polaroid i-Zone instant camera, and the Steelcase Leap chair that is found in just about every office today (the one with the springy back where you can rock back and forth like a corporate grandma). It's also the organization that pioneered design-thinking methodology, a "human-centered approach to innovation" (as opposed to the robot-centered approach to innovation that led to the Matrix).

The design process at IDEO includes many elements you might expect: a diverse team, qualitative research, quantitative analysis, experimentation, rapid prototyping, an iterative approach, and a heavy emphasis on customer feedback. It also includes a few things you might not expect at the center of innovation: play, improvisation, and (not all that surprising, given the topic of this book) humor.

And the process works. Since 1991, IDEO has topped *Business Week*'s annual Industrial Design Excellence Awards, and in 2005, the magazine named IDEO one of the 20 most innovative companies in the world.

"What makes [our team meetings] work is the enthusiasm, the show-and-tell, the humor, the irreverence," Tom Kelley, former CEO of IDEO, shared in *The Art of Innovation*. "The secret, I think, is to scuttle rules, provide good food, and encourage lots of play."

IDEO isn't alone in its use of humor for innovation. Engineering schools like at Purdue University now provide improv classes to help students turn obstacles into opportunity. Corporations like Procter & Gamble and Mattel have established innovation programs that have a big emphasis on fun. I launched a book out of a catapult because of a joke I wrote.

Whether it's designing the next big idea or solving the problem at hand, humor can be a valuable tool for thinking smarter.

The What of Thinking
. . . .

The next skill after being able to execute is being able to think—assess a situation and analyze it, create a plan of action to achieve an outcome, and build a strategy for long-term success. If executing is about doing the work, thinking is about defining the work that should be done.

Some strategists place thinking before execution. After all, you have to know what task to do before you can do it. But the truth is, as an individual, execution comes first. Most entry-level positions are about completing the tasks assigned by others, and not every role requires a high cognitive load. Cooking fries or pulling shower doors, while hard work in their own right, aren't about strategic problem-solving but efficient execution.

But roles are changing, and the ability to think is becoming more important at all levels. Studies suggest that between 35 to 55 percent of all business failures are attributed to strategic blunders. According to a World Economic Forum survey of chief human resources and strategy officers, complex problem-solving and critical thinking are the top two skills needed for success in the 21st century, along with being able to respond to messages with the perfect gif and knowing how to floss (both the dental care technique and the dance).

Success at work isn't just about what you do but is also about how you think.

Critical and Creative

There are a lot of misconceptions about the brain. The notion we only use 10 percent of it has long been debunked, despite any 2014 movies starring Scarlett Johansson that claimed otherwise (I mean, good grief, *Lucy*). The idea that the left brain is for analytical thinking and the right brain is for creativity is also misconstrued—both sides work together for almost all tasks, and individuals don't actually have a bias toward one or the other. And the fact that my bigger forehead means I have a bigger brain turns out to be something I made up to make myself feel better.

While the brain is a fascinating thing to study—according to neurobiologist Bruno Dubuc, if each hemisphere of the brain were unfolded, they would be the size of an extra-large pizza—I am no neuroscientist and this is no brain book. So rather than focus on thinking, fast and slow, we're going to focus on the two primary modes of thinking in the workplace: critical and creative.

Critical thinking is the objective analysis and evaluation of an issue in order to form a judgment. Creative thinking is looking at something in a new way. Critical is convergent, creative is divergent. Critical is logical, sequential, and objective. Creative is intuitive, imaginative, and subjective. Critical is knowing I should eat more salad. Creative is adding chicken nuggets to the salad so I actually eat it.

While people often feel like they lean toward one mode, critical or creative, the reality is both are needed to get results. Consider the five-step problem-solving cycle:

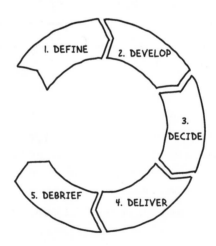

1. Define the problem.
2. Develop ideas.
3. Decide on a plan.
4. Deliver the solution.
5. Debrief the results.

Both modes of thinking are at work in these steps. Defining the problem, picking the solution, creating the plan, and reviewing the process all involve critical thinking around the problem and the solution. Brainstorming possibilities is clearly a creative endeavor, but creativity can also help move each of the other steps along the way. For example, exploring the validity of an idea by putting it "on trial" can be a creative way to decide on a plan (and gives you a chance to finally live out your dreams of being a hot-shot attorney like Harvey Specter in *Suits*).

The key to thinking smarter is being able to think both critically and creatively.

Critical Thinking

You walk into a room where you find a table pushed against the back wall. On the table sit three items: a book of matches, a box of tacks, and a candle. There are no birthday cakes or vigils in sight.

Above the table is a corkboard. Your instructions are to affix the candle to the corkboard in such a way that when you light the candle, no wax will drip onto the table or floor beneath it. You have 10 minutes to complete the problem. What's the solution?

This is a famous scenario known as the candle problem that has been used in hundreds of studies, including one to understand the impact humor has on problem-solving. Students were split into three groups: one of the groups watched a comedy film (a TV show of bloopers), one watched a neutral film (about math), and one watched no film at all. They were then presented with the candle problem.

The number of subjects who watched the humor film and successfully completed the task was 55 percent higher than the neutral film group and 62 percent higher than the group that watched no film at all. Said differently, the subjects who watched the humor film were nearly four times more likely to solve the problem (and probably in a better mood; I mean, I love math, but bloopers are also pretty great).

Why did experiencing humor before solving the problem increase the chances of coming up with a solution? Because of how humans think.

The Paradox of Choice

The primary function of critical thinking is to make a choice. You analyze a situation so you can decide on what action, if any, to take. The more options you have, the harder deciding can become, what psychologist Barry Schwartz calls the paradox of choice.

This is why in sales they say a confused mind says no. The primary purpose of sales is to help customers make a decision. Sales expert and author of *Exactly What to Say* Phil M. Jones says the job of a salesperson can be simply described as "professional mind-maker-upper." But when faced with too many options, the easiest decision is often not to make one at all.

Think about deciding where to eat. Sometimes you'll ask a significant other where they want to go for food and they'll say,

"I don't care." "Okay, how about Chipotle?" "No." "Potbelly?" "No." "Five Guys?" "No." "But you said you don't care!" "I don't." The question "Where do you want to eat" has too many possible answers. Naming a specific place makes it easier to say yes or no.

Every day, we make hundreds, if not thousands, of choices. Some are easy ("Should I have a milkshake? Yes!"). Some are hard ("What kind of milkshake? So many good choices."). And as we make decisions throughout the day, the quality of our decision-making starts to deteriorate, something known as decision fatigue. It's why we're susceptible to impulse purchases at the check-out counter and why I'll have a salad for lunch, fried chicken for dinner, and an entire sleeve of Double Stuf Oreos for dessert.

The consequences of decision fatigue can be very real. Consider one study that found that judges are strongly influenced by how long it has been since their last break, with the percentage of favorable rulings dropping gradually from ~65 percent to nearly zero within each decision session. After the break, the percentage returns back to ~65 percent. It seems unfair that your sentencing is dictated by when your judge last got to go to the toilet, but that may be a factor in the decision.

So how do you combat decision fatigue? Some people try to make as few decisions as possible. Steve Jobs wore the same thing every day, and I used to have a Pop-Tart for breakfast every morning: it was one less choice to start the day. (I have since switched from Pop-Tart to banana to reduce my sugar intake. And that's an actual banana, not a banana-flavored Pop-Tart, which I have to imagine would be disgusting.)

But what if you have a series of important decisions you *have* to make? What if you can't easily limit the possibilities? What if you don't look good in a turtleneck? Critical thinking requires good decision-making skills, in making either the right choices for a long-term plan or a snap decision in the moment on what to do next. To combat decision fatigue and to make sure you're in the right frame of mind for any decision, use humor.

"Humor engages your whole brain," says neurohumorist Karyn Buxman. "When you laugh, it generates a cascade of neurotransmitters, engaging your prefrontal cortex which processes wit, the limbic system which evokes mirth, and the occipital lobe which generates laughter." This full brain engagement improves focus, increases objectivity, and improves overall brainpower. Which leads us to our next humor strategy.

Humor Strategy #3: Spark Insight

This strategy comes directly from what we know about how we recharge (the judges' decision-making reset after a break) and how we can boost our thinking (the students' critical thinking improved after watching humor). The strategy is to take a shot of humor prior to any critical thinking exercise—or as we humorists love to say, go from ha-ha to a-ha.

The next time you have to make an important decision, spend five to 15 minutes doing something fun before jumping in. You can do this alone or with your team, but the key is to experience humor in order to warm up the brain and prepare for the critical thinking task ahead.

Here are three quick ways to do that.

1. Watch something funny.

The easiest way to get laughing is to watch (or listen to or read) something funny. As I mentioned in chapter 4, The Skill of Humor, you don't always have to be the creator of humor. Warming up the brain is a great time to leverage all of the hilarity that already exists in the world by watching a comedian on YouTube, putting on a comedy podcast, or reading anything by

David Sedaris. And yes, that means I am giving you an excuse to watch cat videos if that's what brings you joy.

2. Play something fun.

The second way to spark insight is by playing a quick game. The game shouldn't be too intensive (no Settlers of Catan) but something that can be done quickly and without too much pressure, like a crossword puzzle, a sudoku puzzle, or a jigsaw puzzle. If puzzles aren't your thing, 1) don't try an escape room, and 2) any other game should do (even Candy Crush). Apps like Lumosity and Peak have games specifically designed for warming up the brain.

3. Work something easy.

The last way to warm up the brain is to do an activity that gets you thinking. Simple improv warm-ups like mind meld, the pattern game, and walk/stop can get you ready for the decisions to come.[12]

The exact warm-up you do isn't all that important; just about anything that will keep you engaged and laughing for five to 15 minutes will do. After the boost, you'll be ready to think critically about the problem in front of you ... and you'll be more likely to know how to affix a candle to the wall: remove the tacks from the box, tack the box to the corkboard, and set the candle in the box.

---

12 Read the instructions for these exercises at gethumor.org/activities.

Creative Thinking

. . . .

It was the first day of class and I was nervous. I had taken countless improv classes before, but this was different. This was a musical improv class.

If you're not familiar with musical improv, over the course of 30 minutes you improvise an entire musical, with completely improvised scenes, songs, and sporadic dance moves. I had signed up for the class to learn how to become more emotionally committed in my scenes (being an engineer hadn't really prepared me for expressing emotion on stage).

After some introductions and vocal warm-ups that included singing about mumbling mice, our teacher, the incredible Tara Copeland, got each of us up for "spot songs."

"I'll give you a suggestion, Frank will start playing, and whenever you feel ready, you start singing." Frank was the superbly talented piano player who improvised the background music of our made-up songs.

One by one, my classmates got up and improvised a song on the spot. The topics ranged from pineapples to flamingos, but they all followed the same structure we had just learned:

1. Sing a single line. Repeat that same line three more times to create the four-line chorus.
2. Sing a four-line verse that maybe rhymes but also doesn't have to.
3. Repeat the four-line chorus.
4. Sing a new four-line verse.
5. Return to four-line chorus and end on a big note.

Prior to the class, I had no real understanding of music. I had never sung in public before and I don't exactly have a melodious voice. But those five steps seemed like something even I could do. And when Tara first explained this structure, I thought, *It can't be that simple, right?*

It turns out that it is. And not just for improvised songs but also for songs you hear on the radio. They don't usually follow this exact format, but songs by professional musicians do typically have a structure and there is plenty of repetition. In Justin Bieber's breakout song, "Baby," he says the word "baby" 56 times. In fact, it comprises 21.9 percent of the song. You might say, "But that's Justin Bieber" or "Why do you know that?"

If the Biebs seems like an outlier to you, consider the Beatles. "Hey Jude" has 334 total words but only 58 unique words. The phrase "hey Jude" is said 23 times. The refrain at the end is "Na na na na na na, na na na, hey Jude" repeated for four minutes. It was the band's biggest hit in the US. When it comes to song structure, you have to let it be, let it be, whisper words of wisdom, let it be.

But the structure I learned in my musical improv class didn't stop there: it was in everything we covered over the next eight weeks. Even our completely improvised musicals followed a framework, the same one used in most Disney musicals: opening number, protagonist song, conflict song, friends song, climax, and finale.

To some, this may seem antithetical to creativity. Most people think being creative means being unrestricted and free to choose anything. But there is a lot of structure in creativity, and that structure doesn't make things any less creative—it just makes the process easier.

The Creative Perspective

Creativity, like humor, is often considered innate, something that people are gifted with an ability to do. But the truth is, like humor, anyone can learn to be more creative.

At its core, creative thinking is simply a way of looking at problems or situations from a fresh perspective. Neuroscientists have found that creativity is intrinsically linked to perception, and the most powerful driver of innovation is the ability to think laterally across seemingly unrelated questions, problems, or ideas. Sounds a lot like humor.

As Einstein maybe said, "No problem can be solved by the same kind of thinking that created it." Sometimes the key to solving a problem lies simply in changing how you think about it. Consider this number problem shared in middle school: What is the number of the parking space containing the car?

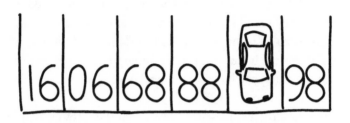

How quickly did you get the answer? If you look at the problem head-on, it seems almost impossible to know: 16 to 6 is minus 10, plus 62 plus 20 ... It's like numbers being called out at the DMV: there's no discernible pattern. But if you change your perspective ...

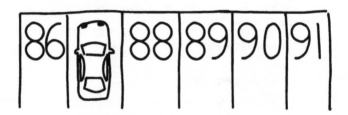

The solution is very easy.

How we view a problem goes a long way in how we solve that problem. But how do we change our perception?

One way is to change our environment. Studies show working outside of the office can increase concentration, improve memory, and remove creative roadblocks. This is why we have some of our best ideas in the shower, a phenomenon known as a creative pause. By doing a menial task that distracts the brain—showering, running, doing the dishes—we think about things differently, which can lead to insights, a-ha moments, and new ways of seeing things.

Shower Thoughts

Some of my favorite "shower epiphanies" from reddit:

- "The brain may have named itself, but it also recognized that it named itself and was surprised when it realized that." /u/gopackdavis2
- "Swans are loud, territorial, violent, aggressive, terrifying, and an emblem of romantic love." /u/Nothingweird
- "They say with pessimism you'll either be correct or pleasantly surprised, but that's an awfully optimistic way to see pessimism." /u/whiteboydrink
- "Someone has your dream job and hates going to work every day." /u/Cien_fuegos
- "Because telescopes work using mirrors, we'll never know if there are any space vampires." /u/Champs27
- "When people think about traveling to the past, they worry about accidentally changing the present, but no one in the present really thinks they can radically change the future." /u/kai1998
- "The only part of your reflection you can lick is your tongue." /u/CardboardDreams

Read more at reddit.com/r/showerthoughts.

Another way to change your perception is through using humor. Humor is highly correlated with both creativity and intelligence. It can also stimulate the brain to set off divergent thinking, allowing you to see broader applications and new perspectives. Which leads us to the next strategy of using humor for creative thinking.

Humor Strategy #4: Improvise Innovation

There are two major misconceptions about improvisation. One is that people think it's often about winging it. It's not. Improv is about leveraging all of your expertise and knowledge in the current moment.

People also think it's about being funny, when it's really about reacting honestly. It's about exploring a point of view—your own or that of a character—so deeply and thoroughly that something new comes forth. That same exploration can be the key to seeing things in a new way and to solving problems that at first seemed insurmountable.

To think more creatively, follow the steps of improvising.

1. Seek inspiration.

As improvisers, we often get inspiration in the form of a suggestion from the audience that then leads to a single scene or an entirely improvised musical. You can find inspiration in the problem you are trying to solve or the circumstances you are trying to improve. Write down (or think about) what you would like to achieve, and use that as your springboard for step two.

2. Apply constraints.

As we talked about with critical thinking, humans suffer from the paradox of choice, and this is particularly true when it comes to being creative. Rather than rambling through any and all possibilities, improvisers apply constraints and form to what they do.

In short-form improv, like on *Whose Line Is It Anyway?* or at *ComedySportz*, improvisers play games with very specific rules—such as having to do a scene by only asking questions or guessing an activity using only gibberish and pantomime. In long-form improv, like at UCB or iO, the show may seem more free-flowing, but improvisers are following specific scene structures and forms such as the Harold (a surprisingly hard-to-describe form) or Fairy Tale Musical (the Disney structure I mentioned earlier).

To enhance creativity in your own work, establish constraints around the problem you defined that you must work within. If it's a challenge at work, look to the requirements. If it's more of an artistic endeavor, create parameters for what you want the end result to be (such as a poem, a painting, or a paragraph of text about the origin of business clichés).

3. Think, If this is true . . .

One of the best ways to find new connections, whether in improv or creative problem-solving, is to deeply explore a topic. Apply a *yes and* mindset and start generating ideas, like Eddie Izzard did with the Death Star cafeteria example in chapter 4, The Skill of Humor. Imagine "if this is true, what else is true," where "this" is an initial thought around the problem. The best place to start is with what is most obvious to you, because that may not be what's most obvious to the other people sitting in the room.

Starting with the obvious removes the need to "be creative." And it works. How often have you seen a comedian point out something obvious but in a way that is unique? We've all heard that it's a small world; it took Steven Wright to point out that you wouldn't want to paint it.

The next time you need creative thinking, try being a little more obvious, and if you're concerned your process is too structured, remember to just let it be.

Thinking with Humor

IDEO helped bring computers into a new era of usability with the work it did on the Apple mouse. Now, more than 30 years later, it's considering where humans will go next as artificial intelligence and machine learning become commonplace. As IDEO CEO Tim Brown recently shared, "As the pace of innovation speeds up, disrupting entire industries, we must hold dear what is uniquely ours: the ability to understand human behavior and creatively solve for human needs."

Machines will continue to replace varying levels of the "execute" tasks humans do today. But being able to think critically and creatively is an important skill for success in any workplace and will be vital to staying employable in the future. It can be the difference between toiling away at meaningless work and strategically executing a plan that delivers results.

To think critically, spark insight and combat decision fatigue while mitigating the paradox of choice. To think creatively, improvise innovation. Leverage your existing expertise to think about the problem in a new way and imagine what else is possible.

Humor can help you make the right decisions at the right time, and it can help you see patterns that solve problems. You determine how you think, so why not use humor?

7

Humor and
Communication

• • •

O N FEBRUARY 19, 2018, I opened my inbox and was
excited to see the following email subject line: *Harnessing Humor for Humanitarian Work: Drew + Red Cross?*
I was excited because that is some excellent alliteration.
And because, while I love the work I do empowering individuals
at corporations all around the world, it's great when I can also
use my talents with nonprofits and community organizations.

Dr. Pablo Suarez, associate director for research and innovation at the Red Cross Red Crescent Climate Centre, sent
the alliterative email because he was interested in exploring
the use of humor in disaster management. I was familiar with
some of Pablo's work as we had met at a conference a few
years prior. He's an avid learner and always seeking innovative

solutions for the humanitarian sector, including turning disaster data into 3D sculptures, playing games for disaster preparedness at the White House, and taking edible insects to a UN conference in Paris. Humor was his next innovation, and I was happy to help.

Over the next few months, we worked together on incorporating humor into his programs. This included some general guiding principles for using humor (what's found in this book), some specific strategies for using humor to improve communication (what's found in this chapter), as well as some one-on-one coaching and script-writing of possible humor to use.

A few months later, I received an update from Pablo after he had delivered a climate workshop to the global Red Cross Youth: *Humor update from Italy:* THANKS DREW!! + *Survey, etc.*

There was no alliteration this time, but the content was even more exciting than the last. In addition to a recap of the event, Pablo shared, "The impact was ... well, simply put: joyful to experience—and effective to get better (serious) results ... I fully see why your company is called 'Humor That Works' :)." He knew that line would make me smile.

Included in his email were the results of their post-event survey. When answering a question about "the amount of humor used in this session," 90 percent of respondents answered that it was "exactly right," 5 percent said it was too little, and 5 percent said it was too much. When compared to similar sessions the participants had previously attended, 64 percent said the amount of humor used was "much more" and 30 percent answered "somewhat more."

As Pablo summarized, "Thus, we can conclude that a very large proportion of participants found that 'much more humor than usual' was the 'exactly right' amount of humor. This is interesting, especially given that a large majority of participants found the subject matter itself inherently 'very serious' and that they found the session content 'very useful.'"

Pablo experienced first-hand the benefit to adding intentional humor when communicating, particularly when the topic is serious and important. As Tami Evans, employee engagement expert and fellow humorist, says, "If you're laughing, you're listening, and if you're listening, you're learning."

The What of Communication

At the most basic level, communication is the exchange of an idea. It's how you get an idea from your head into the head of someone else. It involves two parties, a sender and a receiver, and can be both verbal and nonverbal.

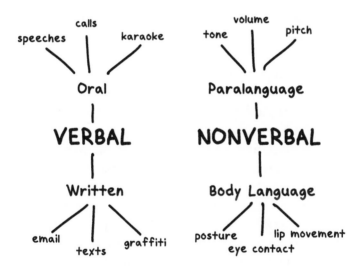

Communication is also one of the most important skills we can master for long-term success. Yes, we have to be able to complete tasks and think strategically, but if we can't communicate with other people about what we're doing and why, we'll be limited in what we can achieve.

Thomas W. Harrell, a professor at Stanford, ran a longitudinal study with Stanford MBA students. The study tracked 150 students over 20 years, ultimately looking for predictors of career success among traits like general energy, thoughtfulness, initiative, self-assurance, and decision-making. The greatest predictor of career success came down to a single trait: verbal fluency.

Harrell defined verbal fluency as "the ability to articulate the intelligence that you have." No, that doesn't mean saying, "Hey, look at me, I'm really smart. Like, *really* smart," but rather being able to communicate ideas in a way that other people understand. He found that the skill was consistently related to career success, whether the student had been out of college for two years or 20.

Professor Harrell isn't alone in his praise of communication. A study performed by the Pew Research Center found that 90 percent of surveyed adults believe communication is the most important skill students should learn. A separate study by Watson Wyatt found that companies that communicate effectively had a 47 percent higher return to shareholders over a five-year period. I assume this is because they don't spend as much time sending passive-aggressive emails that include phrases like "per my last email" and "Sorry for being unclear..."

Communication is something we do constantly. Studies suggest we spend as much as 80 percent of our waking hours in some form of active communication: 9 percent of that time is spent writing, 16 percent reading, 30 percent speaking, and 45 percent listening (although if you believe the stereotypes about millennials, 99 percent of that time is spent texting). And considering things like body language, we are never not communicating. Even sleeping can be a form of communication. Apparently, the way I sleep—on my back with arms crossed—communicates I am a vampire.

But just because we do it often doesn't mean we do it well: 86 percent of corporate executives say that ineffective communication is a big reason for failures in the workplace, and a business with 100 employees spends an average of 17 hours a week clarifying messages, which translates to an annual cost of $528,443.

How can you increase your fluency in verbalness? The key is in how you communicate.

Relevant and Relatable

Imagine through some weird *Encino Man*–style story, a caveperson has been magically transported to today's world (side note: not enough business books reference the 1992 Pauly Shore and Brendan Fraser cinematic masterpiece). Over the course of your conversation with this caveperson, a microwave oven comes up, and you're tasked with explaining it to them. What would you say?

That's the scenario we present in our communication workshops: one participant tries to explain a microwave oven to another who pretends to be a caveperson.

If you're like most of our attendees, you'd explain it by saying things like:

- "It's a box with an invisible fire that cooks your food."
- "It's a rock that's powered by lightning that heats up food."
- "Like small cave. Put wooly mammoth meat in, wait for bird make noise, nom nom nom."

What do you notice? (Besides the last person sounding like Kevin from *The Office*.) The language is simplified, they use terms a caveperson would know, and there's very little science explained. The key to effectively explaining a microwave to a caveperson is the same as the key to effectively explaining anything to anyone, and it boils down to two basic principles: being relevant and relatable.

Relevance is about why the other person should care. Relatability is about connecting what you're saying to what the other person knows. But how do you know what is relevant and relatable to the other person? You have to understand them, you have to ask questions, and you have to actually listen to them. Not "uh huh, sure" listen, but "oh wow, so what you're saying is..." listen.

So often we listen to respond. Someone starts talking, we get a sense of what they're talking about, and then we start to think about how we're going to respond—while they're still talking. Then we're just waiting for them to shut up so that we can drop knowledge on them.

That's very different than listening to understand or, as Stephen Covey described it, "Seek first to understand, then to be understood," one of the seven habits of highly effective people. Listening to respond is an attempt at efficiency; listening to understand is about being effective. And by better understanding your audience, you can communicate in a way that is relevant and relatable to them.

Relevant Communication

Black Friday is the busiest shopping day of the year. People wake up at ridiculous times in the wee hours of the morning to get a jump on all of the best deals. It's when retailers pull out all of the stops to get you to buy, buy, buy with discounts on everything from flat-screen TVs to flatter-screen TVs.

But in 2013, Cards Against Humanity, the makers of the "party game for horrible people," did something truly outrageous: they increased their price on Black Friday and told everyone about it. In a newsletter blast, on their site, and on Amazon, they raised the price of their product from $25 to $30. "Today only! All Cards Against Humanity are *$5 more*."

Next to the offer was a giant *consume* button, and their FAQ offered their reasoning for the price increase:

Why do all of your products cost more today?

We're participating in the tradition of "Black Friday," an American holiday celebrating a time when the Wampanoag tribe saved the settlers of Plymouth Colony with incredible deals. All of our products are $5 more today only, so you can enjoy buying them that much more.

The results were staggering. They were the top post on reddit for the day; got free exposure in publications like the *Guardian*, *AdWeek*, and *Buzzfeed*; and are now a case study in this book (which I'm sure is their proudest accomplishment). As for sales, they were relatively flat compared to the year before (so the $5 increase didn't cost them anything), and they spiked the day after when the price returned to $25. While the entire marketing world was screaming, "Look at me!" Cards Against Humanity got people to pay attention by subverting the norm in a funny way.

They've continued their shenanigans every year, including digging a hole for no reason and selling literally nothing for $5. In 2018, they had a 99 percent–off sale, where they sold various products for 1 percent of their normal costs, including $20 bills for only 20 cents, a signed photograph of Richard Nixon for $6, and a used car for $97.50.

Yes, this one cost them money (unlike raising their prices), but the buzz they gained attracted more than 50,000 visitors to their site over the course of the day and more free exposure all over the internet.

In a world where we are bombarded by information constantly, Cards Against Humanity has found a way to stand out above all of the noise, and you can too.

Paying Attention

According to productivity expert Neen James, we live in an attention deficit society. Citing a study by the Information Overload Group, Neen says, "$588 billion is lost every year in US businesses because of interruptions. We don't have a time management crisis; we have an attention management crisis."

Distractions are everywhere. Every day, the average person sends and receives 112 emails, is exposed to more than 5,000 advertisements, and touches their cell phone 2,617 times. (I would call it a caress but I don't want to make things weird.)

If you want to get people to pay attention, if you want them to look up from their phones and acknowledge your existence, you have to tell them why they should care. Not why you care, but why they should. In marketing, this is the idea of leading with benefits over features so customers can answer the biggest question on their mind: "What's in it for me?" (The second biggest question is, "How will this look on Instagram?")

This gap between why you care and why they should can lead to what Chip and Dan Heath, the authors of *Made to Stick*, call the curse of knowledge. The curse of knowledge is the idea that once you've learned something, it can be difficult to remember what it was like not knowing that thing. We often tell people everything we know, rather than just what they need to know.

I once led a communication workshop for a team at Raytheon. I didn't know this, but Raytheon invented the microwave. So when we got to the aforementioned caveperson/microwave exercise, they were impressed. "Did you do this exercise just because we invented the microwave?" We do that exercise with almost every group, but I still responded, "Absolutely."

The problem some of the people at Raytheon had was that they knew so much about a microwave, they couldn't explain it in terms that a caveperson understood. They were trying to explain that actual microwaves go through the air and cause the molecules in food to vibrate, and that friction causes it to heat up. A caveperson doesn't need to know any of that; they just need to know "makes food hot."

What's relevant to one person might be completely different than what's relevant to another. That's why Aristotle proposed three methods of persuasion: ethos (character), pathos (emotion), and logos (logic). But there's one thing that tends to be relevant to all humans: having fun ("humos," perhaps?). That's because humor creates instant relevance.

Not too long ago, I was speaking at a conference in Munich, Germany. Half of the speakers presented in English, the other half presented in German, a language I do not speak. Normally I try to listen to all the other speakers, especially when I'm the closing keynote, but I found myself tuning out all of the German speakers because I had no clue what they were saying. Except for one.

I listened to almost every word that neuroscientist Henning Beck said, despite it being in German. Why? Because he was making the audience laugh. And even though I had only a fraction of an idea of what he was talking about, I wanted to have fun too. I soon started laughing with the audience, even when I wasn't sure what we were laughing about. That's the power of humor.

This is why starting with humor is so valuable. Sylvie di Giusto, image expert and author of *The Image of Leadership*, says you have seven seconds to make a first impression. If you can make someone laugh in that first impression, they'll listen a little longer. If you continue to entertain and engage them, they'll continue to listen. Because the consistent use of humor keeps people coming back, it makes your brand (whether personal or business) continually relevant.

As Jerry Seinfeld says, "There is no such thing as an attention span. People have infinite attention if you are entertaining them." It's why "busy" people still have time to binge-watch all of *Daredevil* season 3 despite the fact that they should be working on a certain book... And why our next humor strategy is one of the best ways to create relevant communication.

Humor Strategy #5: Engineer Surprise

The best humor strategy for getting people's attention is to engineer surprise through incongruity. Incongruity is simply doing something a little different than expected, something that makes people stop and say, "This ain't the usual."

You can do this in a variety of ways. Cards Against Humanity did it by raising their price on Black Friday. Brian Fanzo, the "pager-wearing millennial," does it by always wearing a hat, cool shoes, and a pager while on stage speaking. I did it on the cover of this book by quoting my mom (who, I hope by now you are realizing, is pretty awesome).

There are five primary methods for engineering surprise through incongruity.

1. Get visual.

Visual incongruity is something that stands out to the eye, such as an interesting image in a presentation or splash of color in the wardrobe. For example, my brother, a professor at Texas A&M, wears a unique pair of socks every day of the semester. His students love seeing what pattern, saying, or pop culture reference will appear next on his foot gloves.

2. Effect sound.

Aural incongruity is something that sounds different than everything else, such as changing your voice or playing music at the beginning of a meeting. Silence can also be particularly effective—sometimes the best way to get people's attention is by not talking at all. A longer than usual pause can build suspense as to what you'll say next.

3. Twist speech.

Verbal incongruity is using phrases or wordage that stands out, such as making up words or calling socks "foot gloves." Simply by saying things in a unique way, you can capture people's attention—they're drawn in by the unique turn of phrase. An easy way to do this is by using humornyms (humorous synonyms), such as in job titles—like when crisis management expert Melissa Agnes tells people she's a professional worrier—or in everyday conversation—like the guy who mixed up the cliché and told me we have to "push the stationery."

4. Make moves.

Physical incongruity is using your body in a surprising way, such as walking around the room while you speak or presenting while lying down (something I've seen marketing expert and acclaimed keynote speaker Drew Davis do masterfully). Even a simple shift in body language or facial expression can capture attention. Case in point: you almost always have some type of reaction (positive or negative) when someone winks at you. Where you stand, how you move, and the way you sit can all create additional interest when communicating with people.

5. Subvert expectations.

Logical incongruity is something that appears, at first glance, to break logic, such as raising your prices on Black Friday as an incredible marketing ploy or starting your meeting on time, even if it's to an empty room. I did this at P&G—if I said the meeting started at 9 a.m., the meeting started at 9 a.m. regardless of who was there. Only once did I present to an empty room (and yes it was weird for the first person who came in to see me talking to myself). While it seems illogical, it told my team members that I started on time with or without them. They became more punctual. Logical incongruity involves subverting what is expected while still delivering what is needed.

Regardless of which style you use, incongruity is a great way to capture attention and communicate in a way that is relevant to your audience.

Relatable Communication

In the Lower East Side in New York City, there's an unassuming black door on Clinton Street, a few doors down from the well-known Ivan Ramen restaurant. On the door is a purple logo that reads "Caveat." Past the door, down some steps, and through a hallway lies a first-of-its-kind comedy club in the basement underneath a preschool.

Caveat bills itself as a "speakeasy stage for playful, intelligent nightlife." One of the first shows I saw there was *Science Exclamation Point*, featuring a science lecture from Ruth Angus, assistant curator of astrophysics at the American Museum of Natural History. Her lecture was followed by an improv set from Thank You, Robot, inspired by the information she shared.

During Ruth's lecture on space stuff, she related her research to sci-fi movies. Or, more accurately, she ruined sci-fi movies. For example, Star Wars: "First of all, there are no explosions in space, because there is no oxygen. Second, you can't see lasers. And finally, the Force isn't real." Whoa, the Force isn't real? That's taking it too far, space lady. There's no amount of science that will stop me from pretending the Force is real every time I walk through an automatic door.

Caveat isn't alone in its use of humor to explain the intellectual. Programs like *School House Rocks, Last Week Tonight*, and *Drunk History* all use comedy as a way to make government, politics, and history more interesting. These same strategies can make any message more relatable: all it takes is a little humor.

Understanding How We Understand

What is a euphonium? I could say it's a series of brass alloys bent into various shapes, it has valves on it, and if you blow into it, it makes noise. Or I could say it's like a small tuba.

If you know what a tuba is, you instantly understand, at a high level, what a euphonium is because I related it to something you already know. That's how we understand new concepts: in reference to what we have in our brainspace. Or as smarter people said in *Frontiers in Behavioral Neuroscience*, "As humans, we do not store verbatim copies of experiences in our memory. Rather, we integrate new incoming information from the surroundings in relation to our pre-existing knowledge about the world."

Every human has a set of knowledge that includes things we had to learn, things we wanted to learn, and things we accidentally learned. In school, we had to learn how to do algebra. We may have decided we wanted to learn about all of the characters in the Marvel Cinematic Universe. And we accidentally learned that Taylor Swift is named after James Taylor and loves cheesecake.

If you want to teach someone a new idea, the key is to relate it to something they already know. If you want to learn a concept yourself, you can create your own association for it. This is why mnemonics are so powerful; they connect something that's easy to remember to something that is more difficult.

Some of My Favorite Mnemonics

Mnemonics can help you remember everything from math functions to CPR. Here are some popular, and some unusual, mnemonics:

- MATH, the trigonometric functions:
  - SohCahToa = Sine (opposite over hypotenuse), Cosine (adjacent over hypotenuse), Tangent (opposite over adjacent)
  - **Note:** I say this about once a week for no reason other than it's fun to say.
- MUSIC, the notes on a treble clef:
  - Every Good Boy Deserves Fudge = EGBDF
  - **Or for Millennials:** Every Good Boy Deserves Feedback
- MANNERS, your bread plate/drink:
  - Make an okay sign with both hands. The left makes a lower-case b, the right makes a d, therefore your bread plate is on your left, your drink is on your right.
  - **Note:** Just don't do what I do when I see b on the left and think, *Oh that must mean beverage... what does d mean?*
- TIME, daylight savings time:
  - Spring Forward/Fall Back = Adjust clocks ahead in March and behind in November
  - **Or (in the future):** Hopefully we won't have to do this at all.
- CPR, the rate of chest compressions:
  - Give CPR to the beat of the Bee Gees' "Stayin' Alive."
  - **Alternatively:** (ironically) Queen's "Another One Bites the Dust."
- HUMOR, how to use humor that works:
  - MAP = Medium, Audience, Purpose
  - **Note:** For those of you named Pamela, I'll allow you to call it your Humor PAM.

In order to relate your message to what your audience cares about, you have to truly understand them. This is why every product at P&G has a strategic target and a prime prospect of who will buy the product. Each prospect is given a persona, even a name: "This product is for Sarah. Sarah is between the ages of 25 and 30 years old. She's already had one career but is on her second and is aspiring to do more. She watches these TV shows, listens to these podcasts, and reads these websites."

P&G does all of this research so they know what is relevant and relatable to Sarah, and they know what type of associations will help her understand that the product is for her. Based on past ad campaigns, it seems like their research has concluded that we all like the Olympics (and their fantastic Thank You, Mom campaign) and Tide ("Yep, it's a Tide ad").

One way to make these associations even more memorable is by using humor. I mentioned my brother and his unique socks. In addition to wearing interesting shoe protectors, he's also a fan of *The Lion King*. In his History of Rhetoric and Western Thought course, Professor Dave uses the movie as a way to explain the story of Gorgias and his encomium of Helen through the defense of Scar, the villain of the Disney film. I'll be honest: I have no idea what encomium even means, but I still understand the story of Gorgias because I understand *The Lion King*. Just like Ruth (the space lady) uses sci-fi movies, my brother uses pop culture to help his students understand complex ideas. It works.

Studies have shown humor can facilitate learning in students—74 percent of college students surveyed indicated that they appreciated instructors' use of humor in the classroom as long as it was used constructively. In particular, humor that helps students make sense of the content (such as association) enhances the students' ability to process it, which can lead to greater retention and learning.

By using the next humor strategy, anyone can use humor to make their content more relatable.

Humor Strategy #6: Reference Funny

The reason why people spend their weekend (and money) listening to scientists talk at places like Caveat is because it's fun. It's not your normal boring lecture ending with death by PowerPoint or coma by Keynote. Just about any content can be spruced up by connecting it to something more interesting.

Any time you have to explain a concept at work, whether it be while training on your product or service, describing what you do, or explaining to your boss why their ridiculous request isn't physically possible, referencing funny can be a great way to make your message stick. By connecting any topic to a more interesting one, the audience is more likely to stay engaged.

Creating such an association is a lot easier than most people realize when you follow three primary guidelines.

1. Make it simple.

If the analogy you use takes 10 minutes to describe, it's not going to help you explain the project you're working on. Instead, look for ways to simplify the concept and relate it to things your audience already knows. Mitch Joel, brand hacker and "rock star of digital marketing," does this brilliantly by explaining the "big bad wolf" of business disruption through the three little pigs of transformation, innovation, and transactions. He takes a complex topic (disruption) and relates it to something nearly everyone knows (a children's story).

2. Make it relevant.

When trying to improve understanding, humor for the sake of humor isn't very helpful. You might have a hilarious joke, but if it doesn't help your board of directors understand why you want to spend $50 million on software, it's not going to be persuasive. This is why the advice to "start with a joke" is usually misguided. If the joke has nothing to do with the rest of the presentation, it's more distracting than helpful. If the reason for using humor is unclear, or if its use would otherwise be confusing, connect your humor to your larger purpose and let the audience know why you brought up Taylor Swift (in my case, as an example of accidental knowledge).

3. Make it fun.

If you're doing the hard work of finding an association to explain your topic, you might as well make it fun. You can do this by picking something you're passionate about, picking something you know your audience is passionate about, or referencing pop culture.

Association is a great instance where you don't have to be the creator of humor. Instead, you can connect your idea to content people already enjoy, like my brother to *The Lion King*, the space lady to Star Wars, or me referencing *Encino Man*.

Once you know what association you want to make, simply find the parallels between it and your topic and explain to your audience how they relate. You'll be rewarded with a more engaged audience, a more enjoyable delivery, and an incredibly relatable message.

Communicating with Humor

A few months after Pablo's successful case study of humor, he shared the value of humor at the UN Climate Change Conference in Poland. His focus was on inspiring government officials, development practitioners, funders, scientists, and other participants on how they might improve their own climate work using humor. The feedback was positive and, hopefully by now, unsurprising.

Attendees of the program said it was eye-opening, fun, and funny: 96 percent of respondents said that humor is useful or very useful for humanitarian work, and 93 percent said they were likely or very likely to incorporate humor into their work as a result of the program. When asked what could be improved, one participant responded, "Deploy it globally."

Whether you're an expert in climate risk or budget risk, it doesn't matter how smart you are if you can't explain what you know in a way that other people can understand. The key to verbal fluency is communicating in a way that is relevant and relatable to the other person.

To be relevant, engineer surprise in the way you communicate to get people to pay attention. To be relatable, reference funny to increase understanding and improve long-term memory retention.

Humor can help you get people to pay attention to your message and understand it better. You determine how you communicate, so why not use humor?

8

Humor and Connection

• • •

YOU HAVE A tough day at work, so when you get home, you throw on some music, pour a glass of wine (or, in my case, some chocolate milk), and text a friend to vent about the day. She responds quickly, commiserates with you, reminds you that your favorite ice cream is sitting in the freezer, and even shares a joke to make you laugh.

Your friend isn't a fellow human but a Microsoft chatbot named Xiaoice (pronounced "Shao-Ice"), and every day, millions of Chinese users exchange texts with her about work, life, and everything in between.

"This is what we call an empathic computing framework," explains Di Li, Microsoft's general manager for Xiaoice. "To create an AI framework, you need to choose EQ or IQ. We chose to do EQ first and add IQ later." The result is a chatbot that people treat as a friend, sending her gifts, sharing personal details with her, and (I'm assuming) trying to set her up with someone like Dom, the voice assistant from the Domino's Pizza app.

Xiaoice isn't the only AI with a predisposition for humor. The Google Assistant can tell you a joke, you can play games with Alexa, and Siri can be downright sassy—just say "Hello Cortana" (the name of the Microsoft voice assistant) to her and she'll respond, "Very funny. I mean, not funny 'ha-ha' but funny."

Computational humor, a branch of AI dedicated to teaching computers how to understand and generate humor, has been around since the early 1990s. Since then, we've seen computers that write puns (JAPE), create double entendres (DEViaNT), and detect sarcasm (SASI). Yes, *The Simpsons* did that last one first. We've also seen robots perform stand-up and improv, and we don't seem too far from Marvin the Paranoid Android from *The Hitchhiker's Guide to the Galaxy*.

Why even try to make computers funny? "Because laughter is such a crucial part of what it means to be human," says Gary McKeown, a psychologist at Queen's University Belfast. "We won't have convincing artificial intelligence until our machines can laugh along with us."

Humor is particularly important when it comes to building relationships. "Humor has a way of instantly connecting us with each other," says Vinith Misra, former Watson researcher and technical consultant on HBO's *Silicon Valley*. "We can look at humor as a sort of WD-40 of human interactions."

Which is exactly why humans need to learn humor as well.

The What of Connection

How we connect with people has a significant impact on not only our ability to get things done but our happiness as well. We humans are social creatures; we need relationships to survive. They're also required for every single business that exists. Regardless of your role or industry, relationships permeate your work. Managers, direct reports, peers, clients, suppliers—they're all words for the same thing: relationships. Why are relationships important in business? Because they are business. "Business is still built on people," says Scott Stratten, CEO of UnMarketing and heralded as the ultimate sales and marketing truth slayer. "People do business with people they like, know, and trust. And if you believe business is built on relationships, make building them your business."

If you're a freelance designer and work by yourself at home, you have a relationship with your clients (even if only electronically). If you're a farmer who takes your crops to market, you have a relationship with the buyers. If you live alone in the woods surviving off only the food you find amongst the trees... well, I'm impressed you've stumbled upon this book. And you have a relationship with yourself and possibly some forest creatures.

At the fundamental level, organizations are systems of human relationships. As individuals, we have to execute and think, but in an organization we also have to communicate and connect. Strong connections lead to better work.

Recent studies have shown that strengthening relationships at work improves morale, increases engagement, and leads to greater workplace satisfaction. According to a 72-year-long longitudinal study at Harvard, the happiest subjects were those who sustained meaningful, healthy relationships throughout their life. All humans crave connection (even us introverts—we just also crave that you maybe pipe down sometimes...).

But not all work relationships are created equal—some will propel your career, others will keep you sane, and a few can even be detrimental. A meaningful relationship is characterized as healthy, caring, long-lasting, and of personal significance. It's with a person who helps you grow, is there when you need them, and calls you out when you're being a bit of a nincompoop.

The more you can build these strong, meaningful relationships, the more likely you are to not only succeed but also be more satisfied with your career. But how do you do it?

Emotional and Experiential

According to the late George Levinger, professor emeritus of psychology at the University of Massachusetts, every relationship is in one of five stages:

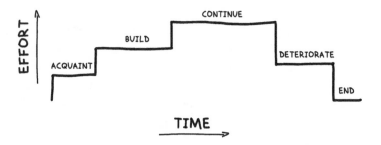

The acquaintance phase is the default stage for most relationships, when people are just getting to know each other. It's the people you've recently met or who you see occasionally—in the hallways, by the water cooler, or awkwardly in the bathroom with that one person on the same schedule as you.

The buildup phase is when you begin creating more comfort and trust with the other person. You'd invite this person to a house party but not your wedding party. In a professional context, this can take the form of the beginnings of a mentorship or as members of a new team or committee.

In the continuation stage, there's a deepening of trust and commitment to the relationship, a corresponding increase in the amount of influence both people can exercise, and an ever greater likelihood that you'll have to drive this person to the airport or watch their dog for a few days. This is the ideal stage to be in with your managers, direct reports, and mentors/mentees after working with them for a period of time. It's also where you'll reap the benefits of better communication, improved productivity, and an increased satisfaction with work.

During the deterioration phase, the relationship starts to become less intimate. Despite its negative connotation, this is often a natural and necessary phase for professional connections. No one works the same job forever, and your level of interaction with certain people is always changing. Without paying special effort and attention to its maintenance, the relationship can revert back to an earlier stage in the personal relationship continuum, end all together, or live in Facebook purgatory where you see their life play out in pictures, status updates, and recommendations for things to do in Paris.

And finally, all relationships end, either through passive lack of contact, intentional breaking of ties, or some other means. Even the contract of marriage states, "Until death do us part."

So what determines the stage you're in with someone? It's often in how you connect with them emotionally and experientially. If you have very little emotional connection with someone and rarely see them, they'll stay an acquaintance forever. As you become more emotionally connected and spend more time together, you'll build the relationship. And once you have a strong emotional connection, you'll stay in continuation even if you don't see that person all that frequently.

I don't talk to my mom every day and I only see her a few times per year, but that doesn't mean our relationship is deteriorating. Our emotional connection and the experiences we've had keep us bonded together. As do the long-distance touch lamps we have.[13] Oh, and the fact that she literally birthed me into this world and is one of the coolest ladies on the planet. It's when the emotions fade and the experiences stop that relationships decline and ultimately end.

Knowing which stage each of your relationships is in, and where you'd like or need it to be, allows you to better leverage your connections for results and happiness. The underlying theme through all of these stages, and the key to connecting closer, is in emotion and experience.

Emotional Connection

The FBI Office of Private Sector is the part of the intelligence branch dedicated to providing an organized, coordinated, and horizontal approach to how the FBI engages with the private sector. In non-government speak, it means they work with companies to provide resources, reduce risk, and (hopefully) prevent them from doing anything that would necessitate an investigation by the FBI. The goal (and their slogan) is to "connect and protect."

They're also one of the most intimidating groups I've ever presented to. Not because they're not nice people, but because 90 percent of them were armed. But it's exactly because of this intimidation that they were interested in learning how to use humor.

A large part of the office's work is in establishing relationships with senior executives to build connection. As you can imagine, having the FBI come up on your caller-ID or appear in your calendar can be a little startling. And some of the

---

13 These are maybe one of the coolest gifts you can give. They are lamps connected via wifi; when you touch one, it lights up the other ones wherever they are in the world. It's a simple way to say, "I'm thinking of you" (or, "It's dark in here").

more typical methods of the FBI—showing up and making demands—don't exactly work for collaboration. The reasons they wanted to learn how to use humor were the same reasons Special Agent Michael reached out about our programs: "I watched a lot of TED talks [when looking for a speaker]. They seemed to be missing something; I found myself zoning out. But when I watched yours, I actually laughed out loud and stayed engaged. Your grandmother is hilarious."

Okay, so maybe the FBI didn't want to learn about humor because of my grandmother, but because they didn't want their contacts to zone out or be intimidated by the FBI (politely) knocking on their door. They wanted to learn humor to build relationships, and that happens when people connect at an emotional level.

The Need for Emotion

When something goes wrong with a computer, you get an error message. You can Google it, do some research, and hopefully figure things out. When something goes wrong with a human, you get "feelings." "Okay Google, why is this person crying?" doesn't usually work.

Admittedly, things would be so much easier if humans came with error messages. If you're working too hard and getting stressed out, it would be great if a message popped up, "Warning: system overload. Please restart by taking a nap." Because taking a nap is the human version of turn it off and back on again.

In lieu of pop-up warnings, humans have emotions. From an evolutionary perspective, emotions exist to get our attention and demand a response. They are our error messages: they're just a lot harder to decode.

Accepting and understanding emotions is the key to updating our mental software and becoming more effective. It's why emotional intelligence is so strongly correlated with success.

Human Error Messages

Things truly would be easier if we had error messages. We wouldn't even have to change the ones that already exist.

- **If you forget someone's name:** "Warning: system out of memory."
- **If you start speeding:** "Caution: illegal operation has been committed."
- **If someone tries to mug you:** "Access denied. You do not have permission to perform this action."
- **If you fall while jogging:** "Failure: runtime error."
- **If you're flirting with a waitress and she isn't feeling it:** "Error: unable to establish connection to server."

In a study published by TalentSmart, 90 percent of top performers had high EQ; less than 20 percent of low performers did. It's no wonder that 71 percent of employers say EQ is more important than IQ and why therapists ask, "How does that make you feel?" not, "How does that make you think?"

To build stronger relationships, empathy is absolutely vital. The ability to understand and share the feelings of another is a fundamental component of what it means to be human. But we also have to understand how we are different.

Many people are aware of the Golden Rule: "Do unto others as you would have them do unto you." It's a fun sentence (you get to say "do unto" twice!) and it seems like great advice on how to treat other people.

As I hope we've all become aware, I love milkshakes. If I've done something to help you out, a fantastic way to thank me is to take me out for a milkshake. I'm not saying you *have* to do something for me, but if you wanted to, a milkshake would be nice. Now let's assume you have done something to help me out. If I follow the Golden Rule, then I would take you out for the biggest milkshake you've ever seen. If you're lactose intolerant, that's not a very good reward.

That's the problem with the Golden Rule: it assumes other people want to be treated the same way you want to be treated. There's a chance they don't. That's why the Platinum Rule is a better way to show respect for someone: treat people the way they want to be treated. Or to make it more fun, say: "Do unto others as they would have you do unto them."

One great way to build empathy with someone and show them you understand them is through humor. Positive humor is positively correlated to high emotional intelligence. And those brief moments of sharing a smile, laugh, or giggle bond us emotionally *and* physiologically. This leads us to the seventh humor strategy.

Humor Strategy #7: Generate Empathy

By learning more about someone and sharing more about our-selves, we can build stronger relationships and show empathy toward each other. This can be done through simple conversation.

As an introvert, I haven't always had the skills needed to chat with people. But as I learned how valuable it was, I took an engineering approach and developed a three-step process for conversation that anyone can follow.

1. Ask compelling questions.
Dale Carnegie is famous for saying that the easy way to be a good conversationalist is to encourage the other person to talk and be a good listener. He claimed you would make more friends in a week by being interested in other people than in a year of trying to be interesting.

The problem is that if you ask the same boring questions, you'll get the same boring answers. That's not really a conversation but a performance of things you've already rehearsed. Instead of the normal, boring questions, incorporate a little humor and ask questions that are different, effective, and fun. Instead of "What do you do?" try "What's the coolest thing you've worked on recently?" Instead of "Where are you from?" why not "What do you like most about where you live?" Instead of "Hi, how are you?" why not "Do you know where I can find a milkshake?"

The goal is to get the person to talk about something they are passionate about. By asking compelling questions, you get the other person to share more about themselves in a way they don't typically think about.

2. Tell interesting stories.

When people ask you a question, it's not about turning it back around on them. You're having a conversation, not playing 20 Questions. So instead of answering with a one-word response, tell a story. Studies have shown that facts are 20 times more likely to be remembered if told in story form. And don't feel like your story has to be strictly work-related. "Don't just tell people your job title and stop there," says John Garrett, former Big Four accountant turned comedian and culture change expert. "Who you are is more than what you do [for work], and what you do outside of your 9 to 5 is what people will remember."

Your story should be interesting, concise, and actually answer the person's question. You don't want a question about your weekend to turn into the 15-minute saga of how you once had to fend off a bear by singing to it. With the right stories, you can create a deeper bond with the other person by connecting with them through your past and future.

3. Continue the conversation.

How do you know what questions to ask or stories to tell when in a conversation? Simply build off the last thing the person said, even a question like "How about this weather?" You can respond, "Yes... and if you weren't at this event, how would you be enjoying the weather?" which turns a conversation about the state of the atmosphere into one about hobbies.

After the conversation, if you want to continue to build your relationship with that person, find a way to follow up. Stay connected: share an article you read on a topic you discussed, keep them posted on news they might find relevant, or send them something funny you think they'd appreciate.[14]

This simple three-step process can help you get to know anyone at any time, while building an emotional connection along the way.

Experiential Connection

I was sitting at the top of the Marina Bay Sands in Singapore, waiting for the fireworks to start when I heard two very distinctive letters.

"O-H!" came the call. I turned to see a young guy in an Ohio State hat approaching me.

"I-O!" I replied.

"I like your Script Ohio shirt," he said as he shook my hand.

"Thank you, great hat!" I responded.

"I think so. My name is Mike. Mind if I wait for the fireworks with you?"

I didn't mind as I'd spent most of the day introverting and welcomed the conversation with a friendly face. Mike and I

---

14 Need ideas for funny things to send? Check out a list of some of our favorite videos at gethumor.org/laughs.

chatted for the next hour as fireworks boomed over the Singapore skyline. We talked about Ohio, our current travels, and whether or not we could actually chew gum on the island city-state. After the fireworks, we headed to a hawker market and had food so good I broke my own rule and actually took a picture of it. It was a fun night with a new friend, all because of two letters.

For any non-Americans reading the book, it's uncommon for two people to spell a state together as a hello (it would take forever for people from Mississippi). "O-H" "I-O" is a specific call and response that students learn at Ohio State as a way to greet each other, get people's attention, or create noise.

Admittedly, when I was an RA, I hated it. Although it was fun to do in the stadium during football games, you most often heard it at three o'clock in the morning from intoxicated residents. As they would yell it out over and over again, I would think, *Congratulations, you can spell a four-letter state… between two people.*

But now when I'm on the road, I love it. It doesn't matter where I am in the world, if I see someone in Ohio State gear, I can yell "O-H" and I'll almost always hear back "I-O!" It creates an instant connection through the shared experience of the Ohio State University.

Increasing Like Ability

One of the easiest ways to be more likable is to be alike-able, a.k.a. to be like someone else. Building rapport basically means finding ways you and the other person are similar.

Think about your close friends and family: they are like you in some way—you grew up in the same town (or household), like the same sports team, or work at the same job. And they laugh at the same things you do. As Piotr Pluta, a psychologist and humor scholar, says, "When you say someone has a 'good' sense of humor, it usually means they share your sense of humor."

This doesn't mean you don't have a diverse set of friends, or that you should lose your identity and pretend to be someone else when meeting someone new. Rather, one of the quickest ways to build a connection is by finding out what you have in common with a person.

You can connect with other people over a shared location. Did you both grow up in the same town, country, or region? I've found that the farther you are from where you grew up, the larger the region you can call home. When I'm in Cincinnati, I have a direct connection with anyone who went to Princeton High School. When I'm in New York, I connect with anyone from Ohio. When I'm traveling abroad, I connect with anyone from the US. When I take that manned mission to Mars, I'll connect with anyone from Earth.

You can also connect over shared interests. Are there things you both geek out about? This could be TV shows, music, or that one really nerdy hobby you have that you only really talk about on the internet. That means there is value in small talk: it helps you find the things you both enjoy. Personally, I usually get along with other soccer-playing, hip-hop loving, *Doctor Who* fans.

And finally, you can connect over shared experiences. Have you both gone through something similar? That could be having children, serving in the military, or even having just done an activity together. Icebreakers or applied improv exercises can be an easy way to create a shared experience. Even if you both hate the activity itself, you've found a way to connect.

This last one is key. "When people have shared experiences—positive or negative—they become closer," says clinical psychologist Joseph R. Dunn.

It makes sense. If people survive a hurricane together, they'll become closer based on the shared negative experience. They bond over the harrowing challenge they overcame, and it becomes a permanent connection they share. I imagine it's the reason Keanu Reeves and Sandra Bullock get together at the end of *Speed*. The same is true for a team who wins the Little League World Series—not the getting together part, the becoming closer together part. The positive experience creates a memory of working as a team that will strengthen their relationships.

There are plenty of negative or stressful experiences we have with our coworkers: working against a challenging deadline, managing budget cuts, and wanting to tell people to stop replying-all but not wanting to reply-all to say it. So it's important to find positive shared experiences as well, something humor can do very well.

When we laugh or smile together, we become closer. Researchers at University College London and Imperial College London found that positive sounds such as laughter or a triumphant "woo hoo!" can trigger a response in the listener's brain. The response is automatic and helps us interact socially by priming us to smile or laugh, thereby connecting us with the other person. This is fascinating to me. One, that something as simple as a laugh can connect us, and two, what other sounds did they test besides "woo hoo"? Does "yowza!" also cause the response? What about "shazam"? Or "kerfluff"? I think I'd have some type of response if someone looked at me and said, "Kerfluff."

The incredible thing about humor is that it has the ability to turn a negative experience into a positive one, and that makes humor so powerful in conflict resolution. "Research shows that when people in a conflict situation laugh and find the humor in a situation, they are likely to shift from convergent thinking to divergent thinking," says international business speaker and fellow humorist Michael Kerr. "They go from believing there is only one possible solution to seeing other possibilities." Using humor pre-emptively, to build strong relationships, is also key. As improv educator Jon Colby says, "It's easier to have difficult conversations once you've had fun ones."

The next humor strategy helps you build those strong relationships by creating experiential connections.

Humor Strategy #8: Facilitate Joy

While the use of any type of humor can help build relationships (we all like to be around people who are fun), an activity can be a great way to include everyone, build the team, and learn something new together. When you and your cubicle mates laugh over a story together, your team does a short icebreaker, or your entire organization participates in an improvised talent show, you become closer together while doing it.

What activity you do is based on your objective and your skillset as a facilitator. Many of the exercises we use in our programs are considered applied improvisation. We take concepts, ideas, and activities from the world of improv and apply them to improving communication skills, building leadership confidence, and sparking creativity.

One of my favorite exercises for creating connection, Story of Your Name, I learned from Kat Koppett, trainer, actor, and author of one of the seminal works of applied improvisation, *Training to Imagine.* The exercise is simple: you go around the room (or have people do this in pairs) and answer a simple question: "What is the story of your name?"

For example, the story of my name is that I was supposed to be a Joseph. But, after I was born, my parents decided I didn't look like a Joseph. So, they grabbed a baby naming book in the hospital and apparently didn't flip through it very long because they chose Andrew (which I'm quite happy with).

You can pull ideas from any number of sources, such as games you learned at camp, activities from school, and exercises from sports, or you can make up your own. There are also plenty of websites and books dedicated to such activities, often listing the instructions, what the exercises teach, and how to debrief them.[15]

Regardless of the activity, there are four major steps to facilitating a positive shared experience.

1. Create a safe environment.

If people are asked to do something different, they need to feel comfortable taking risks. You do this by establishing some clear ground rules and using an exercise appropriate for the level of trust with the group. If people are meeting for the first time, it's probably not appropriate to play Truth or Dare. But if you're in high school at a party with friends, go for it.

2. Give clear, concise instructions.

You want the participants to know what they need to do and when. Giving them instructions in stages, rather than all at once, is a great way to do this. It can also be helpful to give examples of what you're asking them to do or to demonstrate it for them. If you're facilitating an exercise that you wouldn't want to do yourself, it's probably not a good exercise to use. (That's why our programs have zero trust falls and nothing that involves holding hands.)

3. Allow time to experience the activity.

As the facilitator, it sometimes feels like time is moving slowly. However, as someone doing an activity for the very first time, it takes a minute to understand the rules and get into a rhythm. Give people an opportunity to get into the activity

---

15   Check out suggested resources, including *Training to Imagine*, at gethumor.org/exercises.

and experience the ins and outs of it. Having a timer, such as a clock, stopwatch, or the hourglass sand thingy you stole from Pictionary can keep you from cutting an activity short.

4. Debrief the exercise.

When using an activity to also train an idea, the debrief is the most important part of the experience. You want to make sure the group processes what they learned and understands why they did the activity. Using open-ended questions allows the audience to reflect on the experience and start making the connection to how it relates to their work. You want the audience thinking, *Wow, this will help me tomorrow*, not *What was that all about?*

Using an activity is a natural way to build humor in a group setting, particularly when the activities are playful yet relevant to the group. The interactions between participants create incidental humor moments that help to build experiential connections.

Connecting with Humor

Humor creates connection with people, brands, and even artificial friends—for example, a chatbot named Xiaoice. And if a machine can learn how to use humor, so can you.

Whether you work for the FBI or play in the FIB (the Federazione Italiana di Bocce), relationships are the cornerstone of any business. Building strong connections requires understanding the emotions and experiences of our fellow humans.

To connect with emotion, generate empathy. Follow the three-step conversation process to find shared interests and to tell your own story. To connect with experience, facilitate joy. Lead an activity that will bring laughter and mirth to all of the participants.

You spend 40 hours a week with your coworkers, clients, and suppliers, so you might as well get to know them better. Humor can help you build rapport quickly and bring people closer together. When you think about how you want to create your human connections, why not choose humor?

9

Humor and Leadership

• • •

FEW WOULD ARGUE that the United States has faced a more trying and difficult time than during the American Civil War. The country was on the brink of division, one of the largest civil rights issues of all times was at stake (slavery, not the admission of Kansas as a state), and by war's end, more than 620,000 American soldiers had died. To date, the American Civil War remains the deadliest war in American history, with casualties equal to roughly 2 percent of the US population at that time.

Sure, we have more complex problems now, and challenges abound, but the circumstances surrounding the Civil War have yet to be surpassed.

In 1862, the first full year of the war, President Abraham Lincoln called together a special session of his war cabinet to discuss an incredibly important topic. As people entered the room, Lincoln was reading a book. When the members of his cabinet got settled, Lincoln said, "Gentleman, did you ever read anything by Artemus Ward? Let me read you a chapter that is very funny." He read the chapter and heartily laughed when he finished. No other member of the cabinet so much as smiled. So, to the astonishment of the attendees, Lincoln read another chapter.

Silence again. Lincoln didn't waver; he didn't apologize or feel he was in error. Instead, the 16th president of the United States said, "Gentlemen, why don't you laugh? With the fearful strain that is upon me night and day, if I did not laugh, I should die, and you need this medicine as much as I do."

He continued: "Gentlemen, I have called you here upon very important business. I have prepared a little paper of much significance." That little paper was the first draft of the Emancipation Proclamation, one of the most important documents introduced since the Constitution and Bill of Rights.

Lincoln understood that using humor doesn't mean you think something is trivial. And just because something is serious, it doesn't mean it must be done seriously. Humans are emotional creatures, and managing those emotions is key to long-term success.

If perhaps the most revered president of the United States used humor in the same meeting as announcing one of the nation's most significant documents during one of the most stressful times in the country's history, surely we can use it when things are stressful in the office.

Times feel too serious for humor? The truth is times are too serious not to use humor.

The What of Leadership

Leadership is not a position. It is very possible to be a manager of others and be a terrible leader; look at Montgomery Burns from *The Simpsons* or the coffee mug holding guy from *Office Space*. The terrible manager archetype exists because it exists in companies around the world.

Leadership is a mindset. Specifically, it is a mindset in action. Gary A. Yukl, professor of management and psychology at the University at Albany, defines leadership as a social influence process by which followers are motivated to achieve a positive outcome. It's the ability to inspire people to do something. And it's one of the defining attributes of any employee.

There's a reason leadership is the last of the five work skills: it's the culmination of the other four together. Leaders must be able to execute, think, communicate, and connect with those up, down, and across from them.

It's no surprise that the success—or failure—of a business can be accredited to its leaders. A study published in *Forbes* found that poor leaders lost their company money, good leaders made a profit, and extraordinary leaders more than doubled the company's profit compared to other leaders. It's like the saying (I just made up) goes, "If you want to be well fed, you have to be well led."

A study of more than 20,000 employees found that the number two driver of employee satisfaction was manager quality, just after job-interest alignment. In another study, belief in senior leadership was the strongest factor in workplace engagement.

But leadership is not confined to the titled or the ones with management on their workplan. A 20-year-old new hire is just as capable of inspiring change as the 20-year company man or woman sitting in the corner office. In fact, the new kids are often the ones who spark the change (just look at all the things millennials have supposedly "killed").

It's why John C. Maxwell's first irrefutable law of leadership is the Law of the Lid: "Leadership ability is the lid that determines a person's level of effectiveness. The lower an individual's ability to lead, the lower the lid on their potential." If success and happiness at work are the goal, it's crucial that everyone learns to lead.

Intentional and Inspirational

The majority of my leadership development comes from two places: Procter & Gamble and improvisation.

P&G is a promote-from-within company—all of its senior leaders started at entry, or near entry, level positions and worked their way through the ranks. That means that the leadership development program has to excel in order to ensure the company survives (and it means hiring someone is kind of like *The Last Airbender*, where you wonder if this person will become the *Avatar*, a.k.a. CEO).

Improvisation is about adapting and changing in the moment so that you can proactively reach a desired outcome (usually humor). Combined, improvisational leadership consists of five values needed to lead in an ever-changing world, to lead on your feet.

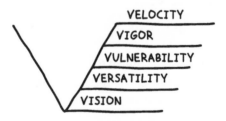

VELOCITY
VIGOR
VULNERABILITY
VERSATILITY
VISION

1. Leaders have vision.

If the goal of leadership is to influence people to take a certain action, you have to know what that action is. "If you want to change what people do," says Tamsen Webster, former executive producer at TEDxCambridge and acclaimed idea whisperer, "you have to change how they see." Simon Sinek has made an entire career out of the value of starting with why. As his book and TED talk so effectively demonstrate, understanding why you are doing something is the key to influencing others to follow.

2. Leaders seek versatility.

As the old management adage states, "If two people think exactly the same, one of them is unnecessary." Bringing together a diverse group of people helps you accomplish the what, why, and how of your vision. But not all teams are created equal. Understanding your teams' strengths and weaknesses, as well as your own, is crucial to leading effectively. As *Motivating Millennials* author Ryan Avery says, "Don't build *a* team, build *the* team." You do that through leadership.

3. Leaders show vulnerability.

To lead with purpose and authenticity, you have to be prepared to share and encourage everyone's humanity. Leadership doesn't mean micromanaging details; it means helping manage the team's energy and well-being for long-term growth and productivity. This means creating psychological safety and building an environment that allows people to be vulnerable. On the best teams, respect precedes results.

4. Leaders encourage vigor.

Change is constant and will happen whether you want it to or not. With change comes the risk of making a mistake or getting things wrong. But failure is just data. Research from Carol Dweck has shown that having a growth mindset—belief that most abilities can be developed through dedication and hard work—is vital to building a team that strengthens over time.

5. Leaders create velocity.

Thinking and doing are two very different things. Leaders actually execute the plan put in place. Action creates more action, and momentum builds as your team reaches milestones and successes, no matter how big or small. Knowing matters; doing matters more.

To achieve these five values as a leader, you have to be intentional about your goals and then inspire humans to get there.

Intentional Leadership

On my first day at P&G, my manager gave me advice that would change my life; he said, "It's better to beg forgiveness than ask permission."

While for some this may be nothing more than a cliché, for me it was an empowering statement. On the first day of my career, he gave me ownership of my work. Over the next few weeks, I thought about the advice.

Being the young, "don't know any better," slightly rebellious new hire I was, I decided to test him. Not by doing anything clearly wrong: I wasn't going to give away company secrets or smuggle loads of toilet paper out of the building. Instead, I did things like sign up for events that new hires didn't normally go to, add jokes to the ends of my emails, and book conference rooms under aliases like Drupac, Winnie the Drew, and Isaac Drewton (incidentally, these are also all rap names of mine).

The one thing I thought for sure would cross the line was declaring myself the corporate humorist of P&G. I got business cards made and started an internal blog. I assumed somebody would eventually stop me. Someone from HR or legal would say, "You can't make up your own job title." But no one ever did. Instead, people started referring to me as the corporate humorist. I'd go to a training and people would be like "Andrew Tarvin . . . wait, are you the corporate humor guy?"

As the self-proclaimed corporate humorist, I set about humoring the organization. I wrote a blog detailing the benefits of humor, taught an improv class to recently hired employees, co-authored a piece with the corporate storyteller, performed stand-up at corporate off-sites, spearheaded a duct-tape fashion show, won internal awards for speaking and training, and even wrote a rap song for the Pringles team ("I'm a Pringles man, with my Pringles can").

For all the song lyrics I used as email subject lines, all the meetings I started with a personal question, and all the projects I gave a fun name to—never once was I told it was too much. Never once did I have to beg for forgiveness, despite actively seeking the bounds to which I could avoid asking permission.

This is only true because P&G lives its values. They expect and want their employees to hold them accountable for the platitudes they preach. But I never would have had the courage to take the risk if they hadn't told me it was okay to do so.

Defining Your Values

The culture of a company isn't defined by its mission statement, the values listed on its website, or the PR it spins in blogs and newspapers. Culture is defined by the way people work, interact, and behave in every single email and every single meeting. As Ron Tite, award-winning creative director and CEO of Church+State, says, "I shouldn't have to read about your values; I should experience them."

As we learned in the chapter on execution, there is a difference between intention and action. Action is the starting point for work and is vital to success. But your intention drives your action; action without intention is leaving success to chance. As Hamilton roasted Burr in the musical *Hamilton*, "If you stand for nothing, Burr, what will you fall for?"

That's why mission statements and team values are important; they serve as the guidepost for how people behave in the workplace. The starting point to living your values is defining them. It's a lot easier to follow a leader who is clear on what they stand for.

The question is: do you know what your company's values are? Are they part of how every employee treats each other or are they in a binder somewhere that you took a quiz on when you first started? Are they even specific to your company or are they generic platitudes that don't really mean anything?

Company values tend to be pretty similar. An analysis by Brand Integrity found the most common values are:

- Teamwork.
- Customer service.
- Integrity.
- Operational excellence.
- Accountability.

There's nothing wrong with those words, but they aren't particularly valuable values. They're the basic cost of doing business. Do you know any companies that aspire for operational mediocrity? While many companies seem to slap together some nice-sounding words, others do stand out with their values (and stand by them).

It's cliché to even mention Zappos, but a humor book can't not include the value "Create fun and a little weirdness." Ben and Jerry's, the ice cream company with an activist heart, has the value to "strive to show a deep respect for human beings inside and outside our company and for the communities in which they live." Warby Parker, the online prescription glasses retailer with a "buy one, give one" donation program, values "creating an environment where employees can think big, have fun, and do good."

The values of these companies match the way they behave. Which isn't always the case. Enron promoted four primary values: communication, respect, integrity, and excellence. They even went as far as to say, "We work with customers and prospects openly, honestly, and sincerely." And then they perpetuated one of the biggest accounting frauds in history. Naming values doesn't guarantee you'll live them, but it is a starting point.

You can also define values for a department or team; they aren't limited to the top-level of an organization or for employees whose title starts with "chief" (corporate or otherwise). Team values help clarify the behaviors you want the people working for you to follow. Building the list out as a group activity can also be a great way to make sure you're building *the* team.

And finally, you can define personal values, the tenets you live your own life by. This allows those who interact with you on a daily basis to know where you stand and how you behave. Personal values can be more specific and action-oriented and can help you define your own legacy. Some examples of my personal values include:

- Err on the side of awesome.
- Be better today than you were yesterday.
- Be more brave than impressive.
- Eat great, even late.
- Stop, collaborate, and listen.

Across all three levels (company, team, and personal), one of the greatest values you can support is humor. As Owen

Hanley Lynch, distinguished teaching professor of corporate communication and public affairs, says, "Organization humor has been linked with successful leadership, with increases in profit and work compliance, with a successful business culture, with message and goal clarity in managerial presentations, with improvement in group problem-solving, and with reducing emotional stress due to threats and role conflict at work."

If you're going to be an intentional leader, why not promote the value that seems to help with just about everything?

Humor Strategy #9: Promote Fun

There are countless ways leaders can be intentional about humor in the workplace and promote it as a valuable skill to learn. The words you say matter a great deal to the people who follow you and to who you follow, so encourage fun as something to strive for.

Here are five ways to promote fun as a value.

1. Lead by Example

One of the ways to encourage humor among others is to use it yourself, particularly if you are in a position of authority or high status. But even if you're not, when you're adept at using humor and it's clear in how it's improving your work, people like Sarah (a.k.a. Ewok) will be inspired. It gives them implicit permission that joy is okay in the workplace, and they'll begin to mirror what they see working.

The flip is also true: if you don't use humor, others won't know it's appropriate. That's often why people don't use humor in the first place—they don't see it happening in the office. You can be the humor spark by using it in your own work.

2. Give People Permission

Another easy step to promoting fun is simply encouraging other people to use it. One way is to simply tell them. Give employees explicit permission to seek ways to improve their own work with a little levity. An even easier way is to laugh more. When someone makes a joke or attempts to use humor, recognize it by laughing, even if it's not the funniest joke in the world. At a minimum, at least smile and share your appreciation for them trying.

The number one reason people don't use humor in the workplace is because they don't think their boss or coworkers would approve. That means if humor isn't used on your team, you're part of the reason why. Change the narrative by expressing your appreciation of humor more. Laughing costs you nothing; it's not like you have a limited reserve and have to save it for something that is "truly funny." Use it for something that's truly important: encouraging humor.

3. Preach the Value

Smart leaders know the value of fun in the workplace. They know the 30 benefits we've mentioned for individuals and the 10 benefits that organizations gain, and they know that 90,000 hours is too much time to not enjoy what you do. Smarter leaders also make sure their people know it as well.

If you know a valuable way for people to be more productive, less stressed, and happier, keeping it to yourself does little to improve the entire team. This isn't Denver: you don't have to stop talking about why it's great because you're worried too many people will move there. Let employees know that not only is having fun okay, it's actually desired as a way to improve the company. Bonus: when your team is funnier, you get to laugh more.

4. Reward Purveyors of Fun

Spotlighting individuals who use humor to be more effective is a great way to create a fun culture at work. Not only does it provide a way to showcase fun that works (allowing other people to share and reapply), but it also encourages people to give it a try so that they too might be rewarded. It's why we run the Corporate Humor Awards every year, to celebrate individuals and organizations who are leveraging humor for better results. It's how I learned about Valve's hilariously written employee handbook, Pixar's 22 rules of storytelling, and HP's banana award (yes, it's just a banana, but it's seen as a great honor).[16]

And don't worry: rewarding fun doesn't require spending money. Giving people a shout-out in the company newsletter, at a company off-site, or even via email can be reward enough for their fun efforts.

5. Tell People How

A majority of people would love to have more fun at work, but many of them don't know how to do it effectively or in a way that is company approved. By training on humor in the workplace, you not only give people permission to use humor, but you also actually tell them how to do it.

Of course, to really deliver the message, you could bring in a professional humor engineer to teach your organization exactly how to have fun while doing their work better (ahem), you could share a book about the subject with them (ahem ahem), or you could do it in your own way.

No matter how you do it, promoting fun as an important value on your team is how you shift the behavior of those around you, and it shows that you lead with intention.

---

16 To learn more, or to learn how to run your own humor awards, go to thehumorawards.com.

Inspirational Leadership

"That's stupid, it'll never work."

That's not the response you're looking for when you've just given a coaching client a piece of advice. I was working one-on-one with Mark, the CEO of a materials manufacturing company, and I had just recommended something a little out of the box for him. Mark was lamenting that he was having a hard time connecting with some of his employees, particularly those who were two or three levels removed from him. He had also just recently asked if I knew any knock-knock jokes that he could share with his kids, who couldn't get enough of them.

My suggestion that was so stupid it would never work was that he start his monthly all-hands meetings with a few of his kids' favorite knock-knock jokes.

"Okay, it may sound stupid, but you hired me to help you find ways to connect. Try it at your next meeting. If you still think it's stupid, I'll refund your money and find you another coach."

That's quite the stakes to put on some knock-knock jokes, but I had a feeling it would work.

A few weeks later, after Mark's next all-hands meeting, I asked how it went. "Should I be refunding your money?"

"I really didn't think it would work," Mark replied. "And I still think it's silly. But it wasn't stupid. I gave them a little background like you suggested and told them my kids love knock-knock jokes, so I thought I'd share a few. I told the first joke and there was an awkward silence followed by polite laughter. I shared the second one and it got a better response, and then I shared the third one and I was shocked by how many people laughed.

"I even added, 'If you know any good ones that I should share with my kids, let me know.' After the meeting, I had five different people come up to me to give me jokes, three of whom were more junior in the company and one of which was a new hire."

Favorite Knock-Knock Jokes

Here are a few of the knock-knock jokes Mark has shared with his team.

Knock! Knock!
Who's there?
Little old lady.
Little old lady who?
I didn't know you
    yodeled!

Knock! Knock!
Who's there?
Boo.
Boo who?
No need to cry,
    it's only a joke.

Knock! Knock!
Who's there?
To.
To who?
To whom!

Knock! Knock!
Who's there?
Déja.
Déja who?
Knock, knock.

Knock! Knock!
Who's there?
Noah.
Noah who?
Noah good knock-knock
    joke?

Knock! Knock!
Who's there?
Orange.
Orange who?
Orange you sick of these
    knock-knock jokes?

Mark has gone on to make the knock-knock jokes part of every all-hands meeting. Its value is not in the jokes themselves, though there are a few great ones. The value is that it humanizes Mark to his employees. He reminds them that he is a father before he's a boss. And it gives people at all experience levels an opportunity to engage with him.

What Truly Inspires

Have you ever experienced impostor syndrome? Ever doubted your accomplishments or capability, worried you'll be exposed as a "fraud"? An estimated 70 percent of people will feel it at some point in their lives.

I occasionally doubt myself before speaking to large audiences—I've never won an Olympic medal, climbed Mt. Everest, overcome a physical disability, survived a natural disaster, or starred in a movie. I'm not a celebrity or an athlete or the CEO of a billion-dollar company. I don't have a TV show and I've never been on *So You Think You Can Survive an Amazing Race*. Why would companies pay me to speak to their people?

But as Adlai E. Stevenson said, "It's hard to lead a cavalry charge if you think you look funny on a horse." As a leader, you have to project confidence and make people believe that you're someone worth following. But you also want to be authentic.

If we see someone as too perfect, too great, or too everything, we can get down on ourselves. We might think, *I could never do that because I'm not attractive or talented or I don't have a cool British accent.* Sometimes, the best way to be inspirational is to be aspirational. I don't want people in my audiences to look at me and think, *I could never do that.* I want them to think, *Well if he can do it, surely so can I.*

Showing that you are imperfect, that you make mistakes and are human, is a great way to build stronger relationships with your coworkers and encourage them in their own struggles. So is using humor.

Warren Buffett was born in 1930, is one of the wealthiest people in the world, and has the cool nickname "the Oracle of Omaha." I was born in 1984, I am not one of the wealthiest people in the world (yet), and the best nickname I've had was Silk, given to me by my bowling coach because I was so smooth. It would seem hard for me to have much in common with Warren Buffett. And yet he seems approachable; it seems like he and I would get along. Why? Because I've seen and appreciate his sense of humor.

After the 2008 recession, Buffett explained what happened in a way people could understand: "You only find out who's been swimming naked when the tide goes out. Well, we found out that Wall Street has been kind of a nudist beach." Or in response to the failures of Freddie Mac: "The amount of money they were told to look for would be inadequate. I mean, 5.5 billion at Freddie would be like taking a spoonful out of the Atlantic to try and save the *Titanic*."

He also uses self-deprecating humor. In an interview with CNBC, he was asked, "So that wasn't you? You weren't the one they spotted walking around in Beijing?" Buffett's response was, "No, that must be my double, George Clooney."

Buffett's use of humor isn't accidental: he considers it a key trait in being both successful and happy. And it's particularly relevant for leaders. A study published in the *Harvard Business Review* found, "People who use [humor], particularly in stressful or seemingly one-down positions, are viewed as being on top of things, being in charge and in control, whether they are in fact or not."

In a study of executives at one company, executives rated "outstanding" used humor more than twice as often as those rated "average." Another study found that employees who rated their manager's sense of humor as above average reported higher job satisfaction and were less likely to look for a job within the next 12 months.

Humor is an authentic way to inspire those around us. Which brings us to perhaps the most important humor strategy of all.

Humor Strategy #10: Be Human
. . . .

My guess is that you are a likable person . . . at home. And then something happens when you go into the workplace. You smile less, you sigh more. You get stressed out more easily and have less patience for the people you interact with. You don't have fun. Humor is a part of your daily existence away from the office.

You watch TV shows that make you laugh, you crack jokes with your friends, you tell stories to family members, and you might even be a little silly from time to time (we all sing in the shower and dance in the kitchen, right?). To be more human at work, use more humor at work.

Here are three ways to do it while also enhancing your leadership skills.

1. Use conversational humor.

Some of the funniest moments in life are spontaneous, unplanned interactions with people. Being good at conversational humor means being present in the conversation, not distracted by other people or that electronic rock in your pocket. Use off-the-cuff humor by staying focused on what other people say, having a playful attitude, and *yes and*-ing the moment.

2. Reveal your passions.

One of the quickest ways to get someone else to open up is to open up yourself. Reveal your own passions and prove that you're not a robot or someone who takes themselves too seriously. Talk about what excites you, what you do outside of work, or your kids' favorite knock-knock jokes.

3. Sprinkle in self-deprecating humor.

As we talked about in chapter 3, Defining Humor That Works, self-defeating humor can be a great way to reduce status differentials and build better connections with your team. Just use it sparingly and always deliver it from a position of confidence to strike the right balance of humor and humility.

To humor is to human; do you think it's a coincidence that both words start with "h-u-m"?[17] Inspire the people you work with by being a human in the workplace.

Leading with Humor

On January 1, 1863, six months after his cabinet meeting, President Abraham Lincoln issued the Emancipation Proclamation, legally freeing more than 3.5 million enslaved people. Though it didn't magically right the wrongs of all that had happened or end the war (that wouldn't happen for another two years), the proclamation ultimately led to the Thirteenth Amendment abolishing slavery following the Union's victory over the Confederate States. And its first draft was preceded by humor.

Leadership is all about influencing people toward a common goal, and humor can help you do that whether you are about to announce the Emancipation Proclamation or getting your team on the same page. When you exhibit intentional and inspirational leadership, you make it possible for people to follow.

To be intentional, promote fun. Be an ardent and vocal supporter of using humor to get better results. To be inspirational, be human. Remind people that, at the end of the day, we're all going through a human experience that we might as well enjoy.

Your actions define the type of leader you become, so why not use humor?

---

17 It's totally a coincidence.

10

Success and
Happiness at Work

• • •

L IFE, LIBERTY, AND the pursuit of happiness. These are the
unalienable rights as defined in the Declaration of Independence of the United States.

Work is directly tied to all three. Work can give us meaning, a purpose beyond mere survival, and a way to direct our
efforts to something greater. Work provides the finances we
need to have the freedom to do the things we want, whether
that's paying for Netflix, raising a family, or drinking large
quantities of milkshake. And work is a large contributor to our
happiness—not only from the hours of 9 to 5. How we feel at
the end of a work day affects what we're willing to do when we
get home. Our attitude toward Monday morning affects how
we feel about the weekend. Our work impacts our life and our
life impacts our work.

The promise of this book was to help you achieve success
and happiness at work. We talked a bit about happiness in why

you should choose humor, and it seems safe to assume that if you effectively use humor to execute faster, think smarter, communicate better, connect closer, and lead further, then you will be more successful.

But as we start to wrap up the what, why, and how of humor in the workplace, it's worth talking directly about success and happiness because there are some misconceptions well worth clearing up.

Success before Happiness?

The major misconception about success and happiness is that success precedes happiness. It's the belief that once you achieve a goal or reach a certain status, you'll be happier. If you only got that raise, or landed that job, or had that car, or this, that, or another thing, you'd be content. But that's not how happiness works. Happiness is not a result: it's a way of being.

The truth is happiness precedes success. Those who can find joy in the work they do will be more successful. As Shawn Achor shares in his book, *The Happiness Advantage*, people who are happy at work:

- Experience 37 percent more in sales.
- Are three times more creative.
- And are 39 percent more likely to live to the age of 94.

So how do you be happier?

Your Happiness Setpoint

In positive psychology, there's a concept known as hedonic adaptation or the hedonic treadmill. The idea is that we all have a base happiness setpoint to which our general demeanor returns, regardless of what happens to us.

When we experience something negative, it will lower our mood for a period of time, but we will eventually return to our base. This is called resilience and is a key factor in the survival of our species. If we lose a client, a project, or our job, it doesn't mean we are doomed to be miserable forever. We will bounce back.

But the same is true for when we experience something positive. We will be happier for a period of time, but we will eventually return to our base. It's why success doesn't lead to long-term happiness—when we get that raise, job, or car, we will be happier for a bit. And then we'll adjust to the new norm and the positive effect wears off.

Research suggests that 50 percent of your happiness set-point is determined by your genes. It's hereditary, what you're born with. That you can't change (unless you're like a scientist from Jurassic Park, and even then, look how that turned out).

Another 10 percent of your happiness is determined by what happens to you. This isn't always something you can control, but your decisions can be part of the cause.

Imagine if every time you go to a certain grocery store, there is a person there who berates you, makes you feel terrible, and stresses you out. If you keep going to that grocery store, that decision is part of what causes you to be in that situation.

That doesn't mean it's right or that you should have to change your grocery store because of someone else—the ideal, of course, is that the person doesn't berate you. But, in this case, they do. And if you can't change what happens to you—maybe you can't go to another store; maybe it's the only one you have access to or the only one that sells Graeter's Ice Cream in your area—then the only thing left to do is change how you respond.

And that's the remaining 40 percent of your happiness: how you respond to what happens to you. Maybe you find out when that grocery person isn't there and go then, or you learn how to laugh at the insults they hurl at you, or you kill them with kindness (note: don't actually kill them). You are in control of that 40 percent.[18]

Now imagine that instead of a grocery-store meanie causing you stress, it's your job or a project or a committee you were "volunteered" for. The options remain the same: if you don't enjoy your work, you can either change what you do or change your perspective. "Take control," as Christine Cashen, author of *The Good Stuff*, says. "It's your life. It doesn't matter what happens to you; it's what you do about it."

Research has shown that there are three primary ways to raise that 40 percent of happiness that you control:

1. Increase your gratitude.

Being grateful helps remind you of the positive things in your life while also improving your relationships with other people. The key is that the bar doesn't have to be high in terms of what you are grateful for.

One of the easiest ways to do this was introduced to me by Matt Weinstein, founder of Playfair, a company that focuses on bringing fun, diverse, and engaging activities to college campuses all over the US. We were speaking at the same conference when he asked the audience the following question: "When are you happiest that you don't have a toothache?"

We were all a little confused. "When are you happiest you don't have a toothache? When you have a toothache. When you don't have a toothache, you never sit around and think, *I'm so happy I don't have a toothache*. But that is precisely when you should be happiest about it."

That story prompted Matt to come up with a simple exercise: "What's not wrong with your life?" The activity is often facilitated in pairs in his workshop, where two people alternate

---

18 This doesn't account for any mental health issues. If you're suffering from depression, anxiety, or any other mental health concerns, please talk with a professional.

turns asking and answering that question. But it's also a great question to ask when you notice you're feeling down or at the end of each day.

Note that the question isn't "What's great about your life?" or "What is so fantastic other people should be jealous?" It's simply "What's not wrong with your life?" The answer could be any number of things:

- I don't currently have a toothache.
- I delivered a program yesterday that people really enjoyed.
- I got seven hours of sleep last night.
- I'm hungry but have a protein bar right next to me that I'm going to eat.
- I'm reading a book that is changing my life, or at least improving it, or at least making me laugh (I hope).

Studies have found that if you write down three things you are grateful for at the end of each day—three responses to the question "What's not wrong with your life?"—you will increase the number of positive emotions you feel, be more optimistic, and weirdly exercise more. (Who knew humor could help you with your fitness goals?)

2. Find happy people.
Which do you think would make you happier: you receiving a $4,500 pay raise or a stranger being happy? You're a bit a torn, aren't you? The obvious answer seems to be the money, but then you're thinking, *He wouldn't be asking this question if it were the money.*

Well, you're right. A team at Harvard Medical School recently analyzed more than 5,000 people and more than 50,000 of their social connections. They found that if a friend of a friend of a friend (a.k.a. someone you've never met) was happy, you were 6 percent more likely to be happy. That's triple the 2 percent chance of being happier because of a $4,500 pay rise.

Dr. Nicholas Christakis, who led the study, explained that moods "spread like ripples through friends." The closer the connection, the bigger the effect. If it's a friend of a friend who's happy, the odds jump to 10 percent, and if it's a direct friend, 15 percent.

They also discovered that this works for sour moods as well, though not as strongly. Each "unhappy connection" decreased the chance of a person being happy by 7 percent.

Multiple studies have shown that you tend to be the average of the people closest to you when it comes to weight, health, and wealth. Happiness is the same. Positivity can be contagious, so it's important to find people in your life who are happy and bring you joy—and nurture those relationships.

This study also speaks to another important point: your happiness affects those around you. As you find ways to improve your 40 percent, you'll be helping your friends, family, and strangers you've never even met. So, thank you.

3. Use humor.

And no surprise, the third way to increase happiness is by using humor. In the longitudinal study done at Harvard that we talked about in chapter 8, Humor and Connection, researchers found humor was one of the healthiest adaptations to being happy in life.

But you already knew that. I mean, it would be weird if I'd written an entire book on humor and it not be one of the ways. And every word leading up to this one has been meant to help you start using humor.

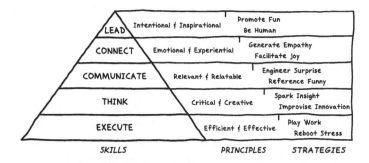

SKILLS	PRINCIPLES	STRATEGIES

What We've Covered

We've covered quite a bit over the last 46,070 words together.

We started with my nerd story in the introduction, covering why I go by Drew (it's the most efficient form of Andrew) and setting the stage for why I wrote this book.

I then kicked things off by talking about humanity's desperate need for humor. With 83 percent of Americans being stressed out at work, 55 percent of Americans being unsatisfied with their jobs, and 47 percent of Americans (and 6 out of 7 dwarfs) struggling to be happy, we realized that the current way of working isn't actually working. Because even though our work has evolved, our approach to it hasn't.

We also covered in detail the What of Work: execution, thinking, communication, connection, and leadership. No matter who you are or what you do, success at work involves mastering some or all of those skills. But to get to the next level, it's not about changing what you do but about how you do it.

Then came the case for why humor should be your *how*. We talked about how humor makes you more productive, less stressed, and happier, and took a look at 30 benefits to using humor in the workplace. We covered the dangers to using humor and why those aren't a good excuse not to use it. It's your life, it's now or never. You ain't going to live forever. Don't you just want to live while you're alive? #bonjovi

Next, we spent some time defining humor to make sure that we were all on the same page. We want to make sure that when Grandma says WTF, we know what she's talking about. We saw that humor isn't about making the workplace funny: it's a way of working that is different, effective, and fun.

We discussed how to make sure our humor stays SFW by avoiding inappropriate topics, targets, or times. We talked about how understanding the four styles of humor—affiliative, self-enhancing, self-defeating, and aggressive—can help you use the right humor in the right place and avoid any unfortunate dongle jokes.

After that, we did a deeper dive into how to actually use humor. We said humor is a skill, which means it can be learned, and that it is made up of your sense of humor, ability to humor, and agency with humor. We also clarified that humor is not, in fact, scarier than living with lions.

First up was sense of humor—or what you find funny, interesting, or curious. Next was the ability to humor—being able to make people laugh or smile by exploring and heightening your point of view and delivering it in a way that people can understand and react to. And finally your agency with humor—how you can leverage humor as a strategy using your Humor MAP of medium, audience, and purpose.

The second part of the book took us deep into the what of work and how humor can be used to elevate each skill.

We started with the foundation of work: execution. You have to be able to git-r-done (à la Larry the Cable Guy). Executing faster requires being efficient and effective, and we can do that by playing our work and rebooting stress.

We moved on to thinking, where the key to thinking smarter is to being critical and creative. We covered how humor can help us do both by sparking insight and improvising innovation. We also learned how to attach a candle to a wall and the number of the parking space containing a car.

Book Stats

In addition to the qualitative look of what we've covered, here's a quantitative look as well.

- Number of Pages: 213
- Number of Words: 53,201
- Number of Unique Words: 6,454
- Number of Characters (Literal): 304,784
- Number of Characters (Figurative): 14
- Number of Footnotes: 21
- Number of gethumor Links: 15*
- Number of References to: work (391), fun (183), happiness (101), success (71), authors/thought leaders (61), comedians (19), puns (17), grandma (16), milkshakes (15), Ohio (15), emotions (12), math (12), movies (11), video games (9), robots (8), zombies (7), wtf (6), orange (5), TV shows (3), reddit (3), dinner etiquette (1)
- First Word (Alphabetically): a
- Last Word (Alphabetically): zoo
- First Word (Chronologically): humor
- Last Word (Chronologically): humorthatworks.com
- Most Frequently Used Word: the (2,252 times)
- Most Frequently Used Pronoun: you (1,038 times)
- Most Frequently Used Noun: humor (663 times)
- Number of Words Used 100 or More Times: 69
- Number of Words Used Only Once: 3,407

* See all of the links at gethumor.org/links.[19]

---

19 Yes, this link is included in the total above. Same thing for this footnote.

Next, we talked about one of the most important skills for long-term success: communication. We said to communicate better we have to be relevant and relatable and use humor to engineer surprise and reference funny. We also ruined Star Wars in the process.

After that was connection and how we can connect closer when we share empathy and experiences, including the effectiveness of "O–H," "I–O." Humor helps us to do both when we generate empathy and facilitate joy.

And then we finally spoke about leadership, the culmination of the other skills, and what is hard to do when you think you look funny on a horse. We said leading requires us to be intentional and inspirational. And humor can help us to improve our leadership skills through promoting fun and being human.

I then started this recap by quoting the object of Nicolas Cage's desire in the movie *National Treasure*—the Declaration of Independence. And we just covered happiness. So, what's left?

Defining Success

"I don't actually want to get promoted."

I was dumbfounded. I couldn't understand what my coworker Tim was talking about. I was in my third year at P&G and had just recently moved to New York City for my next assignment.

"What do you mean you don't want to get promoted?" I asked. "Don't you want to go as high in the company as you can? I know I do."

Tim smiled. "That's not my definition of success. Success to me is having a job that I enjoy and that challenges me. I've got that. It's having the financial stability and means for Judeanne to homeschool our kids and for us to not live paycheck to paycheck. I've got that too. And finally, most importantly, it's having enough time to be active in my family's lives, for me to lead the boys' Boy Scout troop, to attend all of their games, and to put Anna to sleep most nights. And I've got that too.

"If I take a promotion, that means an increased expectation of time at work. It means more stress, managing the careers of other people, and less time for the things that matter most to me."

And just like that, with a little Tim McGilloway wisdom, my understanding of success changed. So often we follow society's definition of success and assume that the goal should always be the bigger salary, the bigger house, the bigger milkshake. But maybe you don't always want the big milkshake; maybe you're already full or you want to go for a run a little later; maybe the small is enough. Or, gasp, maybe you don't even want a milkshake today.

The key to being successful is first defining what success looks like—for you. Not for anyone else, but for yourself. "Living by someone else's definition of success drains your physical and mental energy," says Tracy Timm, a career coach for high-potential young professionals. "When you align your goals with what you do at work, you become rich in every sense of the word."

Phill Nosworthy, CEO of Switch Inc. and one of the best facilitators I've ever seen, describes it so simply: "Most people are working far too hard not to know what they're working for." (Phill was also the first to introduce me to Australia's Tim Tams, so you know he knows his stuff.)

Once you're clear on what success means to you, you can start to work toward it. And if part of your goal is to enjoy whatever it is you want to—or currently have to—do, all the better. Because happiness precedes success. When you find ways to enjoy the work, success will follow.

Of course, none of this really matters if you don't do anything different. My hope is that you enjoyed this book—that it made you smile, think, and laugh out loud at least once so that your coworkers or the people next to you on the train gave you a weird look.

But what matters most to me is that you do something different as a result of these words we've shared. Knowledge is power and, as Uncle Ben taught us, with great power comes great responsibility. So following the transitive property, that means that knowledge is responsibility.

And now that you have this knowledge to add humor, it's your responsibility to go out and use it. As Stephen Covey says, "To know and not to do is really not to know."

I mean, imagine if Superman wasn't a superhero. If he had his super powers but was just regular Clark Kent, mediocre reporter at the *Daily Planet*, churning out clickbait articles all day:

> Find Out What Mineral Lex Luthor Says Will Keep You Safe from Your Enemies
>
> This One Trick Could Help You Leap Tall Buildings in a Single Bound
>
> 20 Signs You're Actually an Alien from a Planet Called Krypton. #7 Will Surprise You

It would be a waste of everything that he was capable of. As I said of effective leaders: knowing matters, but doing matters more.

You have the knowledge, you understand the mindset, and you know the strategies. It's now a choice. What will you do differently now that you've read this book?

Action Items

Naturally, I have some suggestions. Because at the end of the day, I'm still an engineer. As a project manager, I know that everything has to begin with an agenda, a.k.a. the table of contents, and end on next steps. I just call them action items because I think it sounds cooler.

Your primary action item is to start. Which I know is a terrible action item; it's vague and doesn't even come close to following the SMART goals framework (though it does at least rhyme).

But it is the truth. You decide every single day how you're going to do your work, and no one else can change that. You are responsible for your own happiness. The question is: will you actually take charge of it?

Throughout the book, I've shared various examples of things you could do—from reading emails in an accent in your head to telling knock-knock jokes to your team. And each one of the humor strategies has an implicit action embedded: do that strategy. But if you're still at a loss for where to start, I've got a process for you (... that should not be a surprise by this point).

The Humorization Process

For some people, this may seem like overkill or you might think it takes the joy out of finding joy. For those people, feel free to skip to the next section—I think you'll like it. But for the more systems-oriented people out there, these are the steps we go through when working with clients to make sure they're using humor that works.

1. Define the situation.

Think about an area of your work where you'd like to see improvement or that you want to make more fun. Be as specific as possible. You may very well want to make *all* of life better, but start with something a little less existential. Maybe you want to improve your sales numbers, build better relationships with your direct reports, or feel less stressed.

Define the situation around that improvement area, using the Humor MAP:

- What is the medium for this work? How will it be executed?
- Who is the audience for the work? What do they know, what do they need, and what do they expect?
- What is the purpose for using humor to do the work? What do you hope to achieve?

2. Develop ideas.

Once you have your MAP, brainstorm ways you could use humor to achieve your desired outcome. Feel free to do this in the shower if you're in need of that creative pause. If it's helpful, return to the chapter in this book that deals with the primary skill involved. If you want to increase sales, go to communication. If you want to build better relationships, go to connection. If you want to stress less, go to execution.

I also have an entire book on 501 ways to use humor across the five skills, so if you need ideas, take a peek in there. Remember: you don't have to be the originator of the humor. You can share humor that others have created. Always remember to give proper credit, and don't violate any copyright rules. And if you're still at a loss, you can always hire someone to help.[20]

3. Decide on an idea.

Once you have your list of possibilities, it's time to choose an idea. There are a few things worth confirming when making your decision:

- Does it work for your medium, audience, and purpose?
- Does it have an appropriate topic, target, and time?
- Does it make you smile?

---

20 Check out the No Excuses Resources at the end of this book.

Don't forget to use the newspaper rule/Drew's mom test when determining the appropriateness of the idea. And the final question above is particularly important: the more we enjoy the work we do, the more likely the audience is going to enjoy it as well.

4. Deliver the humor.
For some, this is the most intimidating part, but it's also the most fun: executing the humor. Get it out there and see the reaction. To do so:

- **Set the stage appropriately.** Depending on the MAP, it may be important to let people know what's about to happen. Other times it might be weird: "I'm going to tell you a joke so that hopefully you like me more."
- **Deliver confidently.** Own the fact that you're using humor and do it with pride.
- **Connect to your purpose.** This isn't always needed, but if the use of humor is going to seem weird to the audience, tell them how it connects to your primary goal. Again, maybe don't say, "I told you that joke. Do you like me more now?"

5. Debrief the process.
Finally, reflect on the results and the entire process to figure out how to improve.

- Did you have fun?
- What worked well?
- What can be improved?

This review process is key to long-term success: reflection on the past leads to action in the future.

You may have noticed that this process is basically the same as the five steps to problem-solving in the thinking chapter.

That's because that's what a humor engineer does: solve problems using humor.

When you are first starting out, this will likely be a deliberate process that you have to consciously think through. But over time, with practice and repetition, it becomes a natural way of thinking. If you're still not quite ready for five steps, you can start even more simply.

Bonus Humor Strategy: Drive One Smile Per Hour

Maybe you're tired of processes or you don't want to think that much about using humor; you want to just do it. Or maybe you want something easy to remember. Whatever the case may be, I'll leave you with one last bonus strategy.

Simply stated, the One Smile Per Hour strategy is to consciously do one activity every hour that brings a smile to your face or the face of someone else. That's it.

It could be starting a meeting off with a funny anecdote that's related to your presentation, or maybe it's sending a *Parks and Rec* gif in response to a text. It might be as important as listening to a comedy podcast on your way home from work, so that you relieve stress and show up more present for your family, or as simple as smiling at a coworker as you pass by in the hallway.

You can certainly create more elaborate plans for leveraging humor: use the Humorization Process or execute any of the strategies we talked about in the book. Or you can start with a simple habit that you do every day: one smile per hour.

There you have it, 11 strategies for achieving success and happiness at work. It's now up to you to start.

Be Patient Zero

Mahatma Gandhi said, "Be the change you wish to see in the world." Margaret Mead said, "Never doubt that a small group of thoughtful, committed citizens can change the world." And zombies say, "Braaaaiiiiinnnnnnnsssssss."

It turns out we can learn a lot about change from zombies. In fact, our college programs often end on a game called Zombie Tag: one person starts out as a zombie and slowly the entire group becomes the walking dead. What's the point of this, aside from getting people to run around like they did when they were kids?

Because a zombie apocalypse is a great demonstration of how ideas spread. Change starts with a patient zero. A single person who is inspired by an idea (or infected with a brain-eating disease), whose passion (or penchant for biting people) spreads that idea to a small group of people around them. That group (or horde) then shares it with the people around them. And that continues until the idea has spread through an entire team, organization, or family (or the entire population).

You have an opportunity to improve not just your work but also the work of everyone around you. Why not be patient zero?

Every single day you choose how you're going to do your work, so choose to be more productive, less stressed, and happier. Choose to get better results and have more fun. Choose success and happiness in the workplace. Choose Humor That Works.

III

DEBRIEF

. . .

Conversations with the Editor, Part III

"Well, you're finished with the book. How does it feel?"

"Almost."

"You almost feel something? Wait, do you really not have emotions? You just finished a book!"

"I'm almost finished with the book. There are a few more things I want to say."

"Like what?"

"Well, there are a lot of people to thank. I also want to give people some resources so they have no excuses for not using humor. And I should probably prove that I didn't make this all up."

"So, acknowledgments, resources, and sources?"

"You totally get me. Once that's done, I'll feel something."

"What?"

"Proud. This has been the hardest book I've ever written. To put all the work that we've done over the last 10 years with Humor That Works, the last 15 years of being a humorist, and the last 30-plus years of being a sentient human into a coherent, strategic guide was challenging."

"Was it worth it?"

"Absolutely. I've seen the concepts in this book transform teams, organizations, and, most important, the individual lives of the humans who read it. Whether it fundamentally changes how they work or just provides them with a little more joy, I honor the work I get to do every day."

"Well, I think you've done a swell job."

"You're just saying that."

"I'm an editor: I don't 'just say' anything."

"Thank you."

"Not yet—acknowledgments are next. :)"

Acknowledgments

. . .

THIS BOOK WOULD not be possible without the support, ideas, and general awesomeness of so many people. You wouldn't physically have the book if not for the incredible work from the entire team at Page Two Books. To Crissy Calhoun and Jenny Govier for making my ideas stronger and helping me ~~eidt~~ edit this collection of words, Jesse Finkelstein for believing in the idea and in me, Rony Ganon for keeping me on track even when I derailed the schedule completely, Peter Cocking for the design inspiration, and Annemarie Tempelman-Kluit for all of the marketing support. A special shout-out to Sabrina for helping make sure the book was accessible to those beyond the corporate walls and American millennials.

The ideas in this book would not exist without the thought leadership of so many people before me. Of course, much inspiration came from the all-time greats like Dale Carnegie, Stephen Covey, and Peter F. Drucker. Even more came from the contemporary greats, people like Charles Duhigg, Carol Dweck, Thomas W. Harrell, and the entire community of smart speakers and thought leaders I'm privileged to call friends. In the humor space, so much work has been done by Rod A.

Martin, Patricia Ryan Madsen, Mary Kay Morrison, Joel Goodman, and the many authors and experts who are quoted in the previous pages.

These last 10 years would have been a lot weirder and a heckuva lot more boring if not for everyone who has supported Humor That Works. To Raman and Rajiv for all of the business (and emotional support). To Vandad for all the research put in and steps taken to help me grow the company. To the more than 250 clients we've had the privilege of working with, who have provided their stories, served as inspiration, and helped me realize a childhood dream of being a rapper by applauding my poor attempts in my programs. To the countless people who have reached out over the years to tell me of the impact of our work, your anecdotes and stories are the reason we keep going: you're the ones making the change. To Keenan for helping me launch this thing from nothing way back when.

I would have never begun my journey as a corporate humorist/humor engineer if not for the incredible people at Procter & Gamble. Thanks go to Jonathan, my manager when I was an intern, who allowed me to interview so many people and learn about their passions. To John, my manager when I first started, who taught me that it truly was better to beg forgiveness than ask permission. To Pablo for pushing me further than I had been pushed before, professionally and personally. To Hilmar for encouraging my humor in all manner of my work. To Jose for letting me loose on the entire Prestige group. And to Dave, for the encouragement and support to head out on my own.

Thank you to Marni Williams, who started my speaking career by asking me to present on humor to Women in Leadership Networking. To Mike Fulton for making sure it wasn't a one-time thing and continually supporting me throughout the years. To Dan Sullivan for setting up the internal blogs where the *Corporate Humorist* got its first start.

My comedic journey would have never started if not for Nathaniel Sherman, that weird kid from seventh grade who became my best friend and later said, "Let's start an improv group." To Johnny, Moran, Damon, and Chris, who also said yes and helped us build the 8th Floor. To Pat, who has always helped me improve my writing and "punch up" my material. A shout-out to everyone in Smarty Pants and my incredible teachers at UCB and the Magnet, including Bobby Moyhnihan, Zach Woods, Sylvija Ozols, Rick Andrews, Desiree Nash, Tara Copeland, Louis Kornfeld, and Armando Diaz. And, of course, the entire CSZ Worldwide family: Patrick Short, James Bailey, Matt Elwell, Dianah Delaney, and so many more. To Jill Shely, Lynn Marie Hulsman, and Glenn Packman for saying yes to the nerdy kid and welcoming me into the CSZ family.

A huge shout-out also goes to Jeff Jena, my first stand-up teacher, and Jeff Lawrence for creating an incredible community in NYC to practice material. Laughing Buddha Comedy is why many of the jokes in this book exist. And to Caveat for being the home to intelligent nightlife and demonstrating night after night that comedy can be brilliant.

My life would look a lot different if not for my incredible family. To Adam for always being a pillar of support and for psychologically tormenting me just enough that I became resilient. To David for teaching me everything he learned in school and plenty of other things he made up along the way, and for helping me push what Humor That Works could be.

To Dad, who is responsible for my work ethic, my love of math, and a bit of my stubbornness. I think he would be proud of some of the dad jokes that made their way into the book.

To Mom for everything. For the sense of humor, the constant support, the weekly phone calls, and the sanity checks, and for making me the person I am today. And, of course, to Grandma Mary for the optimism, the trolling, and the WTF mindset.

No Excuses
Resources

* * *

OUR MISSION AT Humor That Works is to make the world funnier so that it might be effective-er. We've worked hard to create resources that can help anyone to use humor, no matter what job they have, what level they're at, where in the world they live, how old they are, what skill they start with, or how they feel about puns.

If you make the choice to bring more joy and positivity to this world, we want to support you and we have something for just about any budget.

The starting point is this book. The blood, sweat, and tears poured into these pages were so it can help anyone who wants to make a change for the funnier. Actually, no blood was drawn during the writing of this book, except for when I went to donate blood that one time. I also never got particularly sweaty while working on it, though I did often think through its content while running. And honestly, I only cried once during the creation process, and that's when I thought Google didn't save a draft I had been working on during a flight from Chicago.

But back to you. You decide how you do your work and you are responsible for your own happiness—no excuses. If you still have challenges or don't believe you're able to use humor, we want to help.

If you need more ideas for specific ways to use humor in the workplace, pick up our reference guide *501 Ways to Use Humor*, available in print, on Kindle, and as an app on Android and ios. If you don't have the resources to buy it, send us an email at book@humorthatworks.com and we'll send you the PDF for free.

If you need further inspiration or are looking for funny things related to work, check out humorthatworks.com/fun. It's a repository of workplace-related humor that will make you laugh, smile, or think. All of it is appropriate for the workplace.

If you need help establishing a humor habit, sign up for Humor Shift. This 30-day newsletter course is typically reserved for people who attend our course, but as the owner of this book, you get free access. Go to humorthatworks.com/start, and over the next 30 business days we'll send you an email with three things:

1. A benefit of using humor backed by research, case studies, and real-world examples.
2. A humor challenge to complete that day to build your ability to use humor.
3. Something humorous that will make you laugh or smile that serves as strategic renewal for the day.

If you need support in your humor journey, want guidance on how to use humor in a specific way, or seek feedback on why something worked or fell flat, join the Humor That Works Facebook Group at gethumor.org/facebook. Using humor in a vacuum can be challenging: sometimes you need another opinion. We've created the group to allow people to connect with each other, share ideas, and ask for advice. Myself and other Humor That Works members are active in the group and are more than happy to help.

You can, of course, also hire us. Over the last 10 years, we've developed specific, hands-on programs to help people leverage humor in the workplace. The goal is that this book serves as a guide for you; that with it, you can get started on your own. But I know some individuals and teams want a more hands-on experience. They want to outsource the process and learn in an active environment, with other people on their team or in their department.

We have a wide range of services, ranging from keynote speeches, two-hour workshops, virtual webinars, and full-day humor boot camps. We also offer company consulting and one-on-one coaching for individuals who want to up their humor game.

We try to have something that fits just about every budget, whether that's $0 or a million. If you're committed to using humor to get better results, we're committed to helping you in some way. And if you mention the word "milkshakes" as proof that you've read this book, we'll discount those services by 10 percent.

To get started, visit gethumor.org/strategycall to schedule a free humor strategy call with one of our coaches. We'll learn your humor challenge, give some actionable advice, share a few options, and hopefully leave you with a laugh or two.

We're happy to share all of these resources; we just make one request: share the humor love. We've talked a few different times about the value of an entire organization using humor, and that only happens if there is a culture of it in the workplace. Plus, don't you want the people around you to be funnier so that you can enjoy their humor? Statistically, you'll probably be happier if they do.

Help spread the message that humor is a must-have. Share this book with them. Or order one for your entire team—we do also offer bulk book discounts. If they're not much of a reader, share the audiobook. If you don't think they have the time to read it, share my TEDx talk as a way to start.[21]

If that's still too much of a commitment for them, I have one last option. I've recorded a very special video for people who still aren't on board with humor. In 60 seconds, I cover—very quickly and in about one breath—why humor is so valuable. Send them this link, gethumor.org/whyhumor, as a starting point so that they realize how important humor is. Maybe then they'll be willing to start their own humor journey. Or at a minimum, they won't stop you on yours.

No excuses. The choice is yours.

---

21 Watch the talk at gethumor.org/tedx.

Sources

• • •

1. Humanity's Desperate Need for Humor

American Psychological Association. "Work Stress." Accessed
August 1, 2018. www.apaexcellence.org/resources/
special-topics/work-stress.

Bureau of National Affairs. "Job Absence & Turnover." 2013.

MarketWatch. "People Spend Most of Their Waking Hours Staring
at Screens." Accessed September 12, 2018. www.marketwatch
.com/story/people-are-spending-most-of-their-waking-hours-
staring-at-screens-2018-08-01.

Sorensen, Susan, Garman and Keri. "How to Tackle US
Employees' Stagnating Engagement." Accessed July 14, 2018.
https://news.gallup.com/businessjournal/162953/tackle-
employees-stagnating-engagement.aspx.

2. Why Choose Humor
. . . .

Abel, Millicent H., "Humor, Stress, and Coping Strategies." *Humor* vol. 15, part 4. 2002.

Abramis, David. "All Work and No Play Isn't Even Good for Work." *Psychology Today*. 1989.

Avolio, B.J. "A Funny Thing Happened on the Way to the Bottom Line." *Academy of Management Journal* vol 42. 1999.

Baer, Drake. "Why Humor Makes You More Creative." *FastCompany*. 2013.

Bannister, Steve. "Making Sense of Humour in the Workplace." *Enterprise Magazine*. 2006.

Bennett, Mary P. "The Effect of Mirthful Laughter on Stress and Natural Killer Cell Activity." *Alternative Therapies* vol. 9, no. 2. 2003.

Breeze, Lauren. "Humor in the Workplace: Anecdotal Evidence Suggests Connection to Employee Performance." *Perspectives in Business*. St. Edwards University, 2004.

Cann, Arnie. "Positive and Negative Styles of Humor in Communication." *Communication Quarterly* vol. 57, no. 4. 2009.

Craumer, Martha. "Getting Serious About Workplace Humor." Harvard Business School, C0207D. 2002.

Decker, Wayne H. "Managerial Humor and Subordinate Satisfaction." *Social Behavior and Personality Journal* vol. 15, no. 2. 1987, 225–232.

Dishman, Lydia. "Secrets of America's Happiest Companies." *FastCompany*. 2013.

Einhorn, Cheryl Strauss. "Why Hewlett-Packard is Hiring Dancers." CNN Money. 2013.

Foot, Hugh. "Humour and Laughter." *The Handbook of Communication Skills*. Routledge, 2006.

Fox, Shaul. "The Power of Emotional Appeals in Promoting Organizational Change Programs." *Academy of Management Executive* vol. 15. 2001.

Franklin, Douglas D. "Do Leaders Use Humor." Capella University. 2008.

Garner, Randy. "Humor, Analogy, and Metaphor: H.A.M. It Up in Teaching." *Radical Pedagogy*. 2005.

Ghayas, Saba. "Sense of Humor as Predictor of Creativity Level in University Undergraduates." *Journal of Behavioural Sciences*. 2013.

Griffin, R. Morgan. "Give Your Body a Boost with Laughter." WebMD. 2012.

Humor That Works. "30 Benefits of Humor." Accessed October 20, 2018. www.humorthatworks.com/benefits/30-benefits-of-humor-at-work.

Kerr, Mike. "Putting Mimes to Good Use." *Inspiring Workplaces Newsletter* issue 521. 2014.

Knox, Jill. "Letter from the President." AATH Humor Connection. 2013.

Kurtzberg, Terri. "Humor as a Relationship Building Tool in Online Deal Making." *International Journal of Conflict Management*. 2009.

Lewis, Theodore. "Creativity—A Framework for the Design/Problem Solving Discourse in Technology Education." *Journal of Technology Education*. 2005.

Lynch, Owen Hanley. "Kitchen Antics: The Importance of Humor and Maintaining Professionalism at Work." *Journal of Applied Communication Research* vol. 37, no. 4. 2009.

Lyttle, Jim. "The Judicious Use and Management of Humor in the Workplace." *Business Horizons* vol. 50, issue 3. 2007.

Martin, Rod A. *The Psychology of Humor*. Academic Press, 2007.

McMaster, Robyn. "A Dash of Humor Ups Performance and Creativity at Work." *Brain Based Biz*. 2008.

Mesmer-Magnus, Jessica and Vish Viswesvaran. "A Meta-analysis of Positive Humor in the Workplace." *Journal of Managerial Psychology*. 2012.

Meyer, John C. "Humor in Member Narratives: Uniting and Dividing at Work." *Western Journal of Communications* vol. 61. 1997.

Niculescu, Andreea. "Making Social Robots More Attractive: The Effects of Voice Pitch, Humor and Empathy." *International Journal of Social Robotics*. 2013.

Romero, Eric J. "The Use of Humor in the Workplace." *Academy of Management Perspectives*. 2006.

Sala, Fabio. "Laughing All the Way to the Bank." *Harvard Business Review* F0309A. 2003.

Stauffer, David. "Let the Good Times Roll Building a Fun Culture." *Harvard Management Update* no. U9910B. 1999.

Talbot, Laura, "On the Association between Humor and Burnout." *International Journal of Humor Research*. 2009.

Toffelmire, Amy. "Ha! Laughing Is Good for You!" Canoe.ca. 2009.

Valliant, George E. *Aging Well*. Little Brown, 2002.

Vartebedian, Robert A. "Humor in the Workplace: A Communication Challenge." Presented at Speech Communication Association. 1993.

Wanzer, Melissa B. "An Explanation of the Relationship between Instructor Humor and Student Learning." *Communication Education* vol. 59. 2010.

Warren, Jane E. "Positive Emotions Preferentially Engage an Auditory-Motor 'Mirror' System." *Journal of Neuroscience*. 2006.

Wilkins, Julia. "Humor Theories and the Physiological Benefits of Laughter." *Holistic Nursing Practice*. 2009.

3. Defining Humor That Works

Brooks, Alison Wood. "Research: Cracking a Joke at Work
Can Make You Seem More Competent." *Harvard Business
Review.* 2017.

Cutler, Kim-Mai. "A Dongle Joke That Spiraled Way Out of
Control." *TechCrunch.* 2013.

Kuiper, Nicholas A., and Rod A. Martin. "Three Decades
Investigating Humor and Laughter: An Interview with
Professor Rod Martin." *Europe's Journal of Psychology.* 2016.

Little, Lyneka. "Fired Iowa Civil Rights Investigators
Nicknamed Co-workers 'Psycho' and 'Rainman.'" ABC News.
2011. Accessed July 10, 2018. https://abcnews.go.com/
Business/iowa-civil-rights-employees-fired-catty-emails/
story?id=14362719.

4. The Skill of Humor

Humor That Works. "Survey—How Important Is Humor in
the Workplace?" Accessed September 15, 2010. www
.humorthatworks.com/learning/humor-that-works-
survey-results.

Nihill, David. "Comedy Techniques from the Best TED
Talks." Comedy Habits. 2016. Accessed September
16, 2018. www.7comedyhabits.com/uncategorized/
comedy-techniques-from-the-best-ted-talks.

5. Humor and Execution

Doward, Jamie. "Happy People Really Do Work Harder."
Guardian. 2010. Accessed June 10, 2018.

www.theguardian.com/science/2010/jul/11/happy-
workers-are-more-productive.

EVE Psycho Sisters. "Exoplanets: The Next Phase of Project
Discovery." EVE Online. 2017. Accessed October 8, 2018.
www.eveonline.com/article/exoplanets-the-next-phase-
of-project-discovery. See also https://arstechnica.com/
gaming/2017/05/eve-online-citizen-science-exoplanets and
https://en.m.wikipedia.org/wiki/Eve_Online.

Hanna, Heidi. "The Pros and Cons of Stress with Heidi Hanna."
EO Octane blog. 2015. Accessed September 21, 2018. https://
blog.eonetwork.org/2015/12/the-pros-and-cons-of-stress.

Moran, Brian. *The 12 Week Year*. Wiley Publishing, 2013.

Pattison, Kermit. "Worker, Interrupted: The Cost of
Task Switching." *FastCompany*. 2008. Accessed
June 17, 2018. www.fastcompany.com/944128/
worker-interrupted-cost-task-switching.

Segu, Sashi. "Vacations Recharge Employees' Batteries and
May Help Your Bottom Line." *Innovu*. 2018. Accessed
August 29, 2018.

Sollisch, Jim. "Multitasking Makes Us a Little Dumber." *Chicago
Tribune*. 2010. Accessed June 19, 2018. www.chicagotribune
.com/opinion/ct-xpm-2010-08-10-ct-oped-0811-multitask-
20100810-story.html.

Wachtel, Katya. "The 13 Most Common Reasons You're Likely to
Get Fired." *Business Insider*. 2011.

6. Humor and Thinking

Brown, Tim. "The CEO of IDEO Explains How Your 'Creative
Capacity' Is the Key to Surviving Automation." *Quartz*.
2018. Accessed August 4, 2018. https://qz.com/1260943/
the-ceo-of-ideo-explains-how-your-creative-capacity-is-the-
key-to-surviving-automation.

Buxman, Karyn. "How Humor Can Save the World." TEDxSDSU. May 31, 2017.

Capozzi, Marla M., Renée Dye, and Amy Howe. "Sparking Creativity in Teams—An Executive's Guide." *McKinsey Quarterly*. 2011.

Danzigera, Shai, Jonathan Levav, and Liora Avnaim-Pesso. "Extraneous Factors in Judicial Decisions." National Academy of Sciences of the USA. 2011.

Evans, Lisa. "Working Outside: Why You Should Take Your Work Outdoors." *Entrepreneur*. May 2014.

Gilad, Benjamin. "The Importance of Strategic Competitive Intelligence." Business Strategy Series, Emerald Group Publishing, 2011.

Hauk, William E. "Humor, Creativity, and Intelligence: The Relationship of Humor to Intelligence, Creativity, and Intentional and Incidental Learning." *Journal of Experimental Education* vol. 40, no. 4. 1972.

Isen, Alice M. "Candlestick Problem. Positive Affect Facilitates Creative Problem Solving." *Journal of Personality and Social Psychology* vol. 52. 1987.

Kelly, Tom, and Jonathan Littman. *The Art of Innovation: Lessons in Creativity from IDEO, America's Leading Design Firm*. Edition Publishing, 2001.

———. *The Ten Faces of Innovation: IDEO's Strategies for Beating the Devil's Advocate and Driving Creativity Throughout Your Organization*. Doubleday, 2005.

Naiman, Linda. "What Makes Creative Companies Outperform Their Competitors?" Creativity at Work. 2015. Accessed July 10, 2018. www.creativityatwork.com/2015/01/16/creativity-drives-business-results.

Williams, Terri. "Nearly Half of Millennials Get an F in Critical Thinking." *GoodCall*. 2017. Accessed October 2, 2018. www.goodcall.com/news/critical-thinking-011043.

7. Humor and Communication

Baldoni, John. "How Communication Drives Performance."
Harvard Business Review. 2009. Accessed October 11, 2018.
https://hbr.org/2009/11/new-study-how-communication-dr.

Brod, G., M. Werkle-Bergner, and Y.L. Shing. "The Influence of
Prior Knowledge on Memory: A Developmental Cognitive
Neuroscience Perspective." *Frontiers in Behavioral Neuroscience*
vol. 7. 2013. Accessed July 15, 2018. www.frontiersin.org/
articles/10.3389/fnbeh.2013.00139/full.

Goo, Sara Kehaulani. "The Skills Americans Say Kids Need to
Succeed in Life." Pew Research Centre. 2015. Accessed August
4, 2018. www.pewresearch.org/fact-tank/2015/02/19/
skills-for-success.

Hanson, Bradley A., and Thomas W. Harrel. "Predictors of Business
Success over Two Decades: An MBA Longitudinal Study." Stanford Graduate School of Business, Working Paper 788. 1985.

James, Neen. *Attention Pays: How to Drive Profitability, Productivity
and Accountability*. Wiley Publishing, 2018.

Lee, Dick, and Delmar Hatesohl. "Listening: Our Most Used
Communication Skill." Michigan University Extension. 1993.
Accessed August 5, 2018. https://extension2.missouri.edu/
cm150.

Sanders, G.I. "Employee Productivity Statistics: Every Stat You
Need to Know." Dynamic Signal. 2017. Accessed July 28,
2018. https://dynamicsignal.com/2017/04/21/employee-
productivity-statistics-every-stat-need-know.

Torok, Sara E. "Is Humor an Appropriate Teaching Tool?
Perceptions of Professors' Teaching Styles and Use of Humor."
College Teaching vol. 52, no. 1. 2004.

Whittenberger, Rebecca. "The Problems with Email Communication That Can Be Overcome through Ving." VingApp.com. 2012.
Accessed August 4, 2018. https://blog.vingapp.com/corporate/
via680-infographic-on-the-state-of-email-communication.

8. Humor and Connection

Blanchard, Ken. "Why Are Work Relationships Important?" *Management Leadership* newsletter. October 2010.

Bradberry, Travis. "Why You Need Emotional Intelligence to Succeed." TalentSmart. Accessed October 7, 2018. www.talentsmart.com/articles/Why-You-Need-Emotional-Intelligence-To-Succeed-389993854-p-1.html.

Kerr, Mike. "How Humor Can Help Defuse a Conflict." *Inspiring Workplaces* newsletter, issue 635. 2016.

Krueger, Jerry, and Emily Killham. "The Innovation Equation: Strengths Development + Engagement = Innovation." *Gallup Business Journal.* 2007.

Robert, Christopher. "The Case for Developing New Research on Humor and Culture in Organizations." *Research in Personnel and Human Resources Management* vol. 26. 2007.

Veselka, Livia. "A Behavioral Genetic Study of Relationships between Humor Styles and the Six HEXACO Personality Factors." *Europe's Journal of Psychology.* 2010.

9. Humor and Leadership

Blodget, Henry. "That Awesome Warren Buffett CNBC Interview." *Business Insider.* 2008. Accessed September 19, 2018. www.businessinsider.com/2008/8/that-awesome-warren-buffett-cnbc-interview.

Brand Integrity. "Top 5 Most Common Company Values. Are Yours Here?" BrandIntegrity.com. Accessed June 25, 2018. www.brandintegrity.com/blog/values-unique-learn.

Casserly, Meghan. "What Employees Want More than a Raise." *Forbes.* 2011. Accessed June 24, 2018. www.forbes.com/sites/meghancasserly/2011/12/15/what-employees-want-more-than-a-raise-in-2012/#4796fa6b2f2a.

Gostick, Adrian. *The Levity Effect: Why It Pays to Lighten Up*. Wiley Publishing, 2008.

Maxwell, John C. *The 21 Irrefutable Laws of Leadership*. Thomas Nelson on Brilliance Audio. 2014.

The, Elizabeth. "25 Fascinating Statistics about Employee Engagement." Rise. 2017. Accessed June 24, 2018. https://risepeople.com/blog/employee-engagement-statistics.

Woohoo. "Our Study of Bad Work Days: How Common Are They and What Makes Them Bad?" Woohoo Happiness at Work. Accessed September 6, 2018. https://woohooinc.com/happiness-at-work/study-bad-work-days-how-common-are-they-and-what-makes-them-bad.

Yukl, Gary A. *Leadership in Organizations* (6th edition). Prentice-Hall, 2005.

Zenger, Jack. "Great Leaders Can Double Profits, Research Shows." *Forbes*. 2015. Accessed October 8, 2018. www.forbes.com/sites/jackzenger/2015/01/15/great-leaders-can-double-profits-research-shows/#6412269a6ca6.

10. Success and Happiness at Work

Achor, Shawn. *The Happiness Advantage—The Seven Principles of Positive Psychology*. Currency Publishing, 2010.

———. "Positive Intelligence." *Harvard Business Review*. January 2012.

Christakis, Nicholas A., and James H. Fowler. "Dynamic Spread of Happiness in a Large Social Network." *BMJ* 337. 2008.

Lyubomirsky, Sonja. *The How of Happiness—A New Approach to Getting the Life You Want*. Penguin Books, 2008.

Simon, B. Harvey. "Giving Thanks Can Make You Happier." Harvard Medical School. Accessed July 6, 2018. www.health.harvard.edu/healthbeat/giving-thanks-can-make-you-happier.

Timm, Tracy. "Fixing the Career Myth." Morning Dose video file. July 19, 2018. https://youtu.be/uI1fLsy3jD8.

About the Author

. . .

ANDREW TARVIN IS the world's first humor engineer, teaching people how to get better results while having more fun. Combining his background as a project manager at Procter & Gamble with his experience as a stand-up comedian, he reverse-engineers the skill of humor in a way that is practical, is actionable, and gets results in the workplace.

Through his company, Humor That Works, Andrew has worked with more than 35,000 people at over 250 organizations, including Microsoft, the FBI, and the International Association of Canine Professionals.

He is a bestselling author; has been featured in the *Wall Street Journal*, *Forbes*, and *FastCompany*; and his TEDx talk has been viewed more than three million times. He loves the color orange and is obsessed with chocolate.

For more, visit humorthatworks.com.

CPSIA information can be obtained
at www.ICGtesting.com
Printed in the USA
LVHW091436171119
637608LV00007B/580/P